Praise for The  ind

"If you want to start a business ⌐ ╷╷╷ ┴┴╵ └╵╷╷╷╵╷╵╵ ╵╵╵ have, this is a fantastic resource. Kevin has managed to condense many of the crucial lessons that too many entrepreneurs learn the hard way. Read this book, and you'll be far ahead in the business game."
—**Andrew Dietz**, founder and president, Creative Growth Group

"Kevin stitches together actual life scenarios and outcomes that every entrepreneur needs to understand. This book doesn't live in the clouds like some others do. Real life for real business builders... read it!"
—**Devon Wijesinghe,** serial entrepreneur; chairman, Insightpool; director, Atlanta Technology Angels

"Kevin has just given us the next best *how-to* handbook on starting, building, and sustaining your own business. It is written with such clarity and with commonsense lessons that truly hit the mark, turning complex concepts into simple applications."
—**Kent Matlock**, CEO, Matlock Advertising and Public Relations

"Kevin has done a remarkable job synthesizing the key points about successful entrepreneurship. In valuable detail, he discusses his own enlightening experiences and those of well-known entrepreneurs to help readers get it right the first time. This book is an important resource for current and aspiring entrepreneurs."
—**Eric Overby, Ph.D.**, assistant professor, Scheller College of Business, Georgia Institute of Technology

"*The Entrepreneur Mind* provides an easy-to-understand blueprint for success. It can be used by anyone wanting to make their dream a reality or aiming to take their business to the next level. In this book, Kevin gives key step-by-step principles for building a strong business foundation from idea to execution, and it is truly a must read for everyone ready to step out on faith to start their own enterprise."
—**Samuel T. Jackson**, founder, chairman, and CEO, Economic Empowerment Initiative Inc., and member, U.S. President's Advisory Council on Financial Capability

"Kevin has built a roadmap to success that every entrepreneur needs to read before starting their journey. This book provides a no-nonsense approach to overcoming the roadblocks and detours that are inevitable in entrepreneurship."
—**Chau Nguyen**, founder and CEO, Campus Special

"In this commendable work, Kevin has emboldened a movement very dear to my heart: making entrepreneurship accessible and a viable option for millions of young people around the world."
—**Scott Gerber**, founder, Young Entrepreneur Council; author, *Never Get a "Real" Job*

"An amazing book that reveals the sometimes elusive insights that entrepreneurs need for success, *The Entrepreneur Mind* gets two thumbs up."
—**David Meredith**, president, ePals International

"In our current time, it's essential to share any type of business knowledge that we attain, and Kevin Johnson is definitely playing a pivotal role in contributing to our entrepreneurship age."
—**Vivian Giang**, reporter, *Business Insider*

"The Entrepreneur Mind is a very important contribution to the entrepreneurship literature. One of the critical takeaways deals with relationships, relationships, relationships! To be truly successful as an entrepreneur you must always exceed expectations in all of your diverse relationships!"
—**James I. Herbert, Ph.D.**, professor of Management and Entrepreneurship, Michael J. Coles College of Business, Kennesaw State University

"Wow! Within minutes of reading this book, the business strategies and secrets that Kevin shared more than paid for the price. I highly recommend this book to entrepreneurial newbies, seasoned pros, and everybody in between. Buy it, use it, and watch your business grow!"
—**Shaun King**, founder, HopeMob

"Kevin's book is thought-provoking and insightful. Readers will be challenged on their own beliefs and characteristics regarding entrepreneurship. It is full of rich ideas on how to develop an entrepreneurial mindset and how to build a business the right way, avoiding the issues that have caused others to stumble."
—**Christopher Hanks**, director of Entrepreneurship Program, University of Georgia

"What I absolutely love about this book is the embedded story within about an entrepreneur who sought mentorship, and in turn became a mentor to others. This is an inspiring work from someone I have come to know over the last several years as a continual learner; now Kevin is a teacher whose insights focus on one of my all-time favorite subjects: how to be street-wise. This book isn't just for entrepreneurs, though; it is for thinkers, doers, and winners."

—**Robert Lahm, Ph.D.**, associate professor of Entrepreneurship, Center for Entrepreneurship and Innovation, Western Carolina University

"Kevin Johnson has written a phenomenal book that will inspire readers to become high-achieving entrepreneurs. Cleverly interweaving the lessons from his rich experience with those of business moguls who we all admire, Kevin exemplifies and articulates the great opportunity, fulfillment, and value that pursuing entrepreneurship brings. Well done."

—**Andrew Young**, former mayor of Atlanta, U.S. congressman, and U.S. ambassador to the United Nations

"This book sharpens and focuses the mind of true entrepreneurs! It is an absolute must read for entrepreneurs who are serious about success."

—**Dexter Caffey**, investor, entrepreneur

The

Entrepreneur

Mind

The Entrepreneur Mind

100 Essential Beliefs, Characteristics, and Habits of Elite Entrepreneurs

Kevin D. Johnson

JOHNSON MEDIA INC.

Special discounts on bulk quantities of this book are available to corporations, professional associations, and other organizations. For details, contact Jennifer Rosenberg at
jennifer@johnsonmedia.com or call 404.961.5700.

Johnson Media Inc., Registered Offices:
P.O. Box 4341 Atlanta, GA 30302, United States of America

First published by Johnson Media Inc.

First Printing, March 2013
10 9 8 7 6 5 4 3 2 1

Publisher's Note
This publication is designed to provide accurate and authoritative information in regard to
the subject matter covered. It is sold with the understanding that the publisher is not en-
gaged in rendering legal, accounting, or other professional services. If you require legal
advice or other expert assistance, you should seek the services of a competent professional.

Library of Congress Catalog Card Number: 2012919140

ISBN: 978-0-9884797-0-8

Cover and book design by Johnson Media Inc.

Printed in the United States of America

To the millions of entrepreneurs who, despite daunting odds and grumbling naysayers, start businesses anyway and achieve greatness if only in taking that bold first step.

To my family and friends who have supported me from day one. Specifically, to my wife, Deidre, whose unconditional love includes praising me during success and comforting me during failure, and to my son, Miles, whose smile and laughter are the greatest inspiration for me to pursue my dreams.

Contents

Chapter 2   Education   97

Chapter 3   People   105

Chapter 4   Finance   **133**

Chapter 5   Marketing and Sales   **163**

Chapter 6   Leadership   **193**

Chapter 7   Motivation   **209**

Foreword

The secret of success in life is for a man to be ready for his
opportunity when it comes.
—Benjamin Disraeli, prime minister, United Kingdom (1868, 1874-1880)

While finishing this book, Johnson Media Inc., the small company that I started as a college sophomore in 2000, beat two other companies in a bid for a $40 million project. The project, which spans three years, is the largest account that my company has ever won. Johnson Media Inc. will now be one of the most prominent companies in the marketing industry.

In late July 2012 I received an e-mail and phone call from the vice president of a national organization who was impressed with my company's work in the financial services industry. The vice president asked us to submit a proposal for the organization's major project. I agreed without hesitation.

Although I was on vacation visiting my family in Chicago, I went right to work, summoning my team to focus all efforts on winning this project. Also, I immediately reached out to two mentors whose companies have made millions to get their support and guidance. My team and I finished our winning proposal weeks before the deadline, giving the client the impression that we were all business and that we made their project top priority. It paid off.

I mention this major accomplishment because it is a testament to the effectiveness of the principles discussed in this book. In *The Entrepreneur Mind* I detail how elite entrepreneurs respond quickly, put their business first, consult with mentors often, hire the best team, create an environment of stressful urgency, use time wisely, and so on. The one hundred lessons in this book are precisely the basic principles that I have used to build a multimillion-dollar company at a young age.

This is not just another book on entrepreneurship that focuses on high-level theory or popular thought, but a pragmatic approach that will get you results. In your hands, you have a real playbook to help you accomplish your entrepreneurial dream, whether being able to determine your own destiny or winning a multimillion-dollar account. If you learn from my experiences and the lessons of high-performing entrepreneurs, then you are on the path to success. If you adopt these principles and believe in them wholeheartedly, then success awaits you.

Introduction

To be an entrepreneur is to think differently. While most people seek refuge, entrepreneurs take risks. They don't want a job; they want to create jobs. Their goal isn't to think outside the box as much as it is to own the box. Entrepreneurs don't follow the market; they define the market. This bold and seemingly backward way of thinking I refer to as the Entrepreneur Mind.

How does one develop the Entrepreneur Mind? Debate about this question never ends. Everyone from scholars to entrepreneurs themselves wonder if consciously developing such a mind-set is even possible. Some people believe that entrepreneurs are born, that certain individuals are ordained to be entrepreneurs, gifted at birth with the right mix of characteristics and circumstances. Others believe that entrepreneurs can be developed through a combination of coaching, education, and experience.

The idea that entrepreneurs are born, not made, is ridiculous. Contrary to what many erroneously believe, entrepreneurship *can* be taught and learned. The fact that over six hundred thousand college students were enrolled in some type of entrepreneurship curriculum in 2011, up from less than 1 percent of that amount a decade before, is a testament to the growing belief that entrepreneurship has a respectable place in academia. In many ways, entrepreneurship is like any other major discipline that requires intense study and practical experience.

Although I didn't have the benefit of studying entrepreneurship in a formal classroom setting, I did learn by reading books, many of which I still have in my library and use as references. Trips to the bookstore were a natural first step once I decided to go into business. With teeming excitement and eagerness I bought and read *High-Tech Start Up: The Complete Handbook for Creating Successful New High-Tech Companies* by John L. Nesheim. One of my favorite books was *Netscape Time: The Making of the Billion-Dollar Start-Up That Took on Microsoft* by Jim Clark. Books like these formed the foundation of my education in entrepreneurship. Without them, I would have probably given up from the frustration of trying to figure out everything on my own and to motivate myself.

This book is an attempt to add a fresh and practical perspective to the wealth of knowledge available about how to be an entrepreneur. As I developed as a young entrepreneur and experienced different situations, I realized that few books offered the kind of succinct advice that I now give to my mentees. By telling my personal stories and relating those of other successful entrepreneurs, I set out to write a book that focuses on one hundred core lessons that teach entrepreneurs what they may not find in a textbook, magazine, or online. These lessons range from how to think big to why you should use multiple banks, and even include whom you should choose as a spouse.

Furthermore, my goal in writing this book is to help young entrepreneurs avoid the mistakes I made. Mistakes during the early days of a business can be devastating. A bad decision such as spending too much money or choosing a bad business partner can lead to an entrepreneur having to shut down operations completely. After making some of my biggest mistakes, I would often think, *I wish there were a book out there that would have warned me about this*. Now that book exists, and I can help people who may have that same wish.

This book is divided into seven parts: Strategy, Education, People, Finance, Marketing and Sales, Leadership, and Motivation. Each part contains relevant nuggets of wisdom that you can read separately or sequentially. Feel free to jump around based on your interests or read the book from beginning to end.

Whether you are thinking of starting a business, celebrating your first year in business, or approaching ten years in business, you'll find tremendous value in reading this book. Simply put, it will help you to develop the Entrepreneur Mind.

The

Entrepreneur
Mind

Chapter 1

Strategy

Strategy is a style of thinking, a conscious and deliberate
process, an intensive implementation system, the science
of ensuring future success.
—Pete Johnson, British businessman

All entrepreneurs must ask themselves three vital questions that concern their business strategy: *Where are we now? Where do we want to be? How do we get there?* If you don't know the answers to these questions, you don't have a strategy for success. Instead, you have an aimless, business pursuit and a likely failure on your hands.

Businesses with a clear and a solid strategy are prepared to win. Companies with inferior products often beat companies with superior products because, while the big dogs rest on their laurels, the underdogs are implementing and executing a better strategy. In addition, they may have better partners, employ sharper lawyers, or automate more processes. A company's strategy and tactics can help it surmount what seem like impassible obstacles.

In this chapter, you learn about strategies and tactics to improve your business, ranging from testing a new market to devising an exit plan. Mastery of these important concepts will put your business ahead of the rest.

1) Think Big

It must be borne in mind that the tragedy in life doesn't lie in not
reaching your goal. The tragedy lies in having no goal to reach. . . .
It is not a disgrace not to reach the stars, but it is a disgrace to have no
stars to reach for. Not failure, but low aim is sin.
—Benjamin E. Mays, minister, educator, scholar, social activist

The Two Types of Failure in Business

A business can fail in two ways: not surviving beyond its start and not reaching its full potential. While shutdowns receive the most attention, failure to reach full potential is much more catastrophic.

On the one hand, measuring and understanding why so many businesses fail in the traditional sense is relatively easy. We have the data. Organizations ranging from the Kauffman Foundation to the U.S. Chamber of Commerce have analyzed years of statistics, giving us a solid idea of why about 75 percent of businesses do not survive fifteen years or more. Some of the reasons for failure include undercapitalization, overexpansion, poor planning, and a declining market.

On the other hand, measuring and understanding why a business fails to maximize its potential is quite difficult. Studies and statistics aren't readily available. Also, the default measuring stick for success in business is often the very existence of the business itself. I am guilty of perpetuating this low expectation, frequently congratulating business owners for having survived their first five years. While this accomplishment is honorable, it's more impressive to have a *profitable and a high-growth business* after five years. Instead of flattering business owners who have reached a certain number of years, the goal should be to challenge and to help solid businesses ascend to the next level—to think big.

"Thinking Big" Defined

The phrase "Think big" is ubiquitous, whether it's from an ESPN commentator or Donald Trump. Likewise, a popular T-shirt carries the phrase, "Go big or go home!" Apparently, we have an epidemic of small thinkers, and we must be cured of this contagious inability to think big. Despite its popularity and ascendancy to pop culture status, the saying has no clear meaning, especially as it relates to business.

In business, "thinking big" simply means pursuing ideas that maximize the scope of your potential. Likewise, it can mean pursuing ideas that have maximum impact in the world. Despite its simple definition, thinking big is difficult to do for many reasons, but if you are aware of the obstacles you can avoid them altogether.

1. *One of the main obstacles to thinking big is the inability to outgrow your environment.* I am a mentor to several young entrepreneurs, and one of the common disappointments I have about my mentees is their inability to create businesses that go beyond the confines of their reality or environment. In other words, their environment restricts their thinking to the point that their business suffers limited growth or even death.

To counter this effect I provide examples of entrepreneurs who have gone outside their environment to succeed. For example, many college students wish to start a business that targets only college students on their own campus. Instead, I encourage them to expand their markets by applying their product or service to additional segments. Students, for instance, could sell their product or service to colleges across the nation or the world. If the idea has broad appeal, it could be even larger. Also, I share with my college mentees how Facebook, originally for college students only, was founded on an ideology that appeals to people all around the world. It was just a matter of time before Facebook's cofounder Mark Zuckerberg expanded his company's target from college students to everyone on the planet.

2. *Many entrepreneurs lack the motivation to pursue big ideas.* I find this mentality prevalent among entrepreneurs who have had some level of monetary success in business that diminishes their willingness to pursue bigger ideas. These entrepreneurs strive to maintain their comfort or have become accustomed to going for low-hanging fruit. As business author Michael Gerber says, "Comfort makes cowards of us all." Moreover, these entrepreneurs could simply be overwhelmed with running their own business and don't have the bandwidth to do anything else.

For overcoming lack of motivation, entrepreneurs should find an individual or team to hold them accountable for pursing their big idea, step by step. I know that staying motivated can be difficult. However, having people hold me accountable for my goals has really worked. Moreover, if you have several businesses like I do, you have to delegate tasks to others and carve out priority time to develop your idea. Otherwise, you make little progress.

3. *Several entrepreneurs lack the self-confidence to think big.* They don't see themselves running a large organization, or they are frozen by the immensity of their idea. They may ask themselves, *Where do I start? How will I build a team capable of pulling this off? Where will I get the start-up capital for such a huge idea?*

To boost your self-confidence, devise and take small steps that start you working on your idea. For example, do some basic research about your idea or write down your ideas. If you are like most people, these small wins will add up to increase your confidence and to propel you forward.

4. *Entrepreneurs often lack the diversity and expertise of influencers required to think and eventually to execute in a big way.* I am a fan of the television show *Shark Tank* in which entrepreneurs pitch their business idea to a panel of investors, or sharks, who then decide whether to place an investment with the presenting company. Entrepreneurs who appear on the show seek investment capital as much as the valuable experience of the sharks. In one episode, a shark suggested that an entrepreneur license his product

instead of selling it to individual retailers, an arduous process. The entrepreneur had not thought about licensing his product, a strategy that would yield him profits faster and minimize risk. In this case like so many others, the founder needed the experience and influence of seasoned entrepreneurs to maximize the potential of a business idea.

To jump this hurdle, you must establish a diverse network of individuals who think big and understand what it takes to arrive at that level. Likewise, they can help you to vet and improve your idea. Reid Hoffman, founder of LinkedIn, recently told a group of aspiring entrepreneurs in Cambridge, England, "Talk to as many people as you can. What you want are the people who will tell you what's wrong with your idea. They are the ones you can learn from."

My First Big Idea

Like many of my college mentees today, I was unable to think big during my early start-up days, because I was limited by my environment. Also, my network at the time didn't include older entrepreneurs who could help me translate the value of my college website to a larger, more profitable audience. By the time I realized the great potential of my idea, it was too late. Well-funded and talented competitors seized the larger market aggressively while I focused on increasing my success in my small-college microcosm. Had circumstances been different, I could have been a formidable competitor to companies like CollegeClub.com, or even Facebook itself.

Despite the missed opportunity of becoming a national or even global college web portal, all was not lost. Eager to move on from serving the college market and making my mark in a bigger area, I stumbled upon an opportunity that would forever change how I pursue business ideas. I decided to focus on commercializing an internal tool that I created to help my staff update web pages without having to know computer programming languages. Om-niPublisher, one of the first online content management systems—similar to an early WordPress—was my first product with global appeal. From that point I began to think big and never returned to thinking small.

We sold OmniPublisher to local community newspapers and other publishers to simplify making frequent updates to their websites and to automate archiving with a portable database. OmniPublisher also helped users with small budgets to obtain enterprise-like software that normally would cost them much more to build or to purchase from an established vendor. My company had regional success with the project and eventually sold OmniPublisher to a small publishing company. During an early consolidation period, companies with software similar to my company's were acquired for millions of dollars. My dream of selling to a large media conglomerate at a higher valuation didn't come through, but I sleep well at night knowing that I dreamed big and went for it.

Where Thinking Big Helps the Most

I contend that the aggregate loss of value by businesses that fail to reach their potential is much greater than the value lost by businesses that cease to exist. Some compelling statistics support this position, as reported in a recent Technology Association of Georgia (TAG) proposal:

According to the YourEconomy.org website (created by the Edward Lowe Foundation from Dun and Bradstreet data), from 2000–2007, most new job creations in the United States were provided by Stage I (1–9 employees) companies (approximately 5.7 million). However, over this period of time, new jobs by Stage I companies were created at a rate of 1.5 per new company, whereas Stage II (10–99 employees) companies created new jobs at a rate of 26 per new company. The website further indicates that since 2000, Stage IV (500 or more employees) companies have yet to create one new net job. Instead, they have lost approximately 2.5 million jobs.

For this reason, economists, entrepreneurs, and others interested in economic development should not necessarily emphasize fostering start-up growth. Instead, they must emphasize helping established businesses and leaders transform their operations from medium to large. In other words, increasing the number of new start-ups is less important than ensuring the full maturation of established companies that have tremendous and sustainable growth potential.

How do we move medium-sized businesses to become big enterprises? Many economic developers are asking themselves that question today and are working diligently to answer it. One approach, economic gardening, is addressing the challenge and seeing great results, especially in Florida. As defined by the Kauffman Foundation, *economic gardening* is an economic development model that embraces the fundamental idea that entrepreneurs drive economies. The model seeks to create jobs by supporting existing companies in a community. Economic gardening also develops an entrepreneur's mental ability to think big and provides resources to make it happen.

Making the jump from thinking small to thinking big can be extremely difficult, but it is worth it. In fact, all of the greatest achievements of humanity started with a daring, big idea. Imagine where we'd be if the inspiring words of the great Benjamin E. Mays that encourage us to think big hadn't inspired a young student at Morehouse College who dreamed of living in a different world than the one in which he found himself. Martin Luther King Jr., one of the most known icons in the world today, could have settled for being just a preacher in his hometown of Atlanta, Georgia. He never would have set out to accomplish his dream, a vision that changed our world forever. People with the ability and the audacity to think big carve the path to greatness.

2) Create New Markets

If I had asked people what they wanted, they would have
said faster horses.
—Henry Ford, founder, Ford Motor Company

The two kinds of entrepreneurs are those who create markets and those who do not. On the one hand, the entrepreneur who creates markets is considered a revolutionary. On the other hand, the entrepreneur who competes in well-established markets is considered ordinary. Both approaches can lead to success in business, but research indicates that the creative entrepreneur has a better strategic position.

Blue Ocean Strategy, a best-selling business book, makes a cogent argument that creating new markets known as "blue oceans" is better than competing in overcrowded industries known as "red oceans." The authors, W. Chan Kim and Renée Mauborgne, studied 150 strategic moves spanning more than one hundred years and 30 industries for their book. They also looked at 108 companies that launched new businesses to quantify the impact on revenue growth and profits of creating blue oceans. Kim and Mauborgne's findings are remarkable:

> We found that 86 percent of the launches were line extensions, that is, incremental improvements within the red ocean of existing market space. Yet they accounted for only 62 percent of total revenues and a mere 39 percent of total profits. The remaining 14 percent of the launches were aimed at creating blue oceans. They generated 38 percent of total revenues and 61 percent of total profits.

According to these data, it pays to create blue oceans. The book gives solid examples of successful companies that created new markets, including Yellow Tail, Cirque du Soleil, Ralph Lauren, and Lexus. It also provides a step-by-step process for executing blue ocean strategy. I highly recommend that you buy a copy of the book.

As a mentor to young entrepreneurs, I encourage my mentees to seek new markets rather than to go into well-established ones. The potential for attaining greatness is in creating new markets. My first start-up was a blue ocean, or a blue pond considering the size of my market. In my microcosm of a college campus, I created a web portal that enabled students to interact in ways like never before. As a result, advertisers flocked to take advantage of my platform. Moreover, I encourage my mentees to study some of our greatest and wealthiest entrepreneurs to learn how they were able to identify and to dominate new markets.

Going down the list of *Forbes* magazine's wealthiest four hundred Americans, you read the names of many entrepreneurs who have created and led in markets that before were nonexistent. Michael Bloomberg, for example, started his company after being fired from an investment bank in 1981 and was a pioneer in providing high-quality financial data to Wall Street banks and traders. Before Bloomberg L.P., no company provided this valuable data quickly and in several different formats. Likewise, Jeff Bezos's Amazon.com revolutionized the way consumers buy books and other products. The list continues with names like Michael Dell, Phil Knight (cofounder of Nike), George Lucas, and more.

Which kind of entrepreneur are you? If you have a blue ocean, you are on your way to tremendous success. However, if you are competing in a red ocean, it's time to adopt strategies to spawn innovation, leading your company to significant profits and to a sustainable competitive advantage.

3) Work on Your Business, Not in Your Business

If your business depends on you, you don't own a
business—you have a job.
—Michael Gerber, author, *The E-Myth*

It was one of the greatest feelings of accomplishment and satisfaction I have ever had. After a long and difficult process of searching for the right people, every essential role in my publishing business was filled. No longer did I have to sell ads, do layout, edit articles, or distribute my magazine. My staff of almost twenty people took care of everything from determining a new issue's concept to delivering it to readers. I didn't even have to look at the final printed magazine if I didn't want to. I could now focus on how to grow the magazine from a regional publication to a national one.

Until an entrepreneur's company runs without the founder, that person is just self-employed, the lowest rung in the hierarchy of entrepreneurs. The unfortunate reality for millions of entrepreneurs is that their business depends on them way too much. You know the type, and perhaps that type describes you. They are often overwhelmed with their business, doing everything from their own taxes to taking out the trash. They work nonstop not because they want to but because they have to. They may act as though they have a team that takes care of everything, but they don't. It's all just a façade. The harsh reality is that if they were hit by a bus and died, their business would die, too.

Just because you *have* the ability to assume a crucial role in your business doesn't mean you *should*. In a recent conversation I had, a fellow entrepreneur boasted about his entrepreneurial frugality as if it were an admirable quality. Normally it is, but he took it too far. He enthusiastically bragged, "Why should I pay someone for something I can do myself?" That's usually code for "I don't have money to pay someone else to do the work." If you don't have the revenues to hire a team and to replace yourself, your business isn't profitable, and perhaps you should consider a different approach or a different business altogether. Doing everything in your business yourself leads to a quick burnout, and the activity prevents you from executing your role as an entrepreneur: working on your business, not in it.

Before you even start your business, focus on planning how to get rid of yourself, especially if the business is service-oriented and you are the one serving. This outlook is absolutely imperative because once the business gets going, you won't have time to dedicate to planning when work piles up. You naturally will give priority to serving clients and generating revenue rather than planning your replacement.

Finding quality people to fill all-important roles puts you in the frame of mind of running a business. In this mode, you are really an entrepreneur, and that's what it is all about. Once you have successfully eliminated the dependency of your business on you—and the process won't be quick and easy—you can focus on growing your business or even moving on to your next venture.

I have seen it happen time after time: Entrepreneurs start a company, hoping to be free from the tyranny and demands of a regular job, and before long they are weary from having to do everything for their business. In fact, many are miserable. Either they failed to extricate themselves before it became really difficult to do so, or they just can't seem to let go and get away. If you desire to pass the primary level of self-employment and reach the upper echelons of entrepreneurship, learn to delegate quickly. Otherwise, your chances of growth are limited significantly. If you want guaranteed, limited growth, you might as well get a job.

4) All Risk Isn't Risky

Risk comes from not knowing what you are doing.
—Warren Buffett, businessman, investor, philanthropist

Among the several definitions of an "entrepreneur," some are pretty good while others are downright terrible. Regardless, a common word among them seems to be "risk," which is what truly defines an entrepreneur. The following simple definition by *Merriam-Webster* is one of the best: "An entrepreneur is one who organizes, manages, and assumes the risks of a business or enterprise."

The focus then becomes understanding risk and how it factors into being an entrepreneur. "Risk," as defined by the same dictionary, is the "possibility of loss." What's most interesting about this definition—and contrary to popular belief—is that it doesn't impart a negative value judgment; the definition merely declares the possibility of loss. In other words, an event can have a 1 percent or a 99 percent probability of loss. Our response to and interpretation of those two levels of risk make all the difference.

Entrepreneurs have a higher tolerance for risk than the average person when it comes to starting and running a business. According to the Kauffman Foundation, less than 80 percent of businesses last after their fifth year of existence. Moreover, according to Saratoga Venture Finance, less than 1 percent of businesses ever go public. Despite these daunting odds, entrepreneurs are not deterred from pursuing their goals.

This higher tolerance of risk among entrepreneurs, though, doesn't tell the whole story. Entrepreneurs surely take on high probabilities of failure, but they don't necessarily like to gamble. Instead, they take calculated risks, stacking the deck in their favor. They find ways to minimize or to spread the risk of their endeavor to increase the odds of their success or minimize the odds of loss. Entrepreneurs have the confidence in themselves to avoid and to overcome obstacles that could cause great loss, whether through expert knowledge, solid relationships, or even personal wealth.

For example, the media tend to emphasize the Cinderella stories of CEOs who have achieved great success despite unfavorable odds. However, a closer look at these stories often reveals that the CEOs took calculated risks and had solid backup plans. In his book *The Reluctant Entrepreneur*, Michael Masterson describes how Bill Gates is frequently perceived as a college dropout who took a huge risk to start Microsoft. Masterson criticizes this perspective and paints a very practical picture of Gates, one that portrays him as a methodical, brilliant youngster who always planned to return to school if his business venture didn't work out. Perhaps Gates's decision to leave Harvard would have been riskier and thus worthy of the media spin if he weren't so smart and didn't have the great financial resources that his well-heeled parents gave him.

In short, all risk isn't risky, and entrepreneurs know this rule. Put another way, the reality of becoming an entrepreneur isn't so much about the high probability or risk of failure as much as your ability to beat the odds. Ironically, the entire world has learned this lesson from the Great Recession. The opposite of this rule is just as valid. What people thought was safe is no longer as safe as they thought. College won't guarantee you a high-paying job in the field you studied once you graduate. A corporate job doesn't mean you won't get fired. Enrolling in your company's 401(k) plan doesn't mean that you will have more money in the bank than when you started the plan. If the world continues on a path of economic decline, pursuing your entrepreneurial dreams will be less risky than getting a job. And that's not such a bad thing.

5) Don't Waste Time

Procrastination is opportunity's natural assassin.
—Victor Kiam, entrepreneur; former owner, New England Patriots

I had lunch recently with one of my mentees who just graduated from college. Now that school is occupying less of his time, he wanted to meet and get some guidance about what to do next. He and a couple of his friends from college started a company over a year ago that finally seemed to be gaining some traction.

Although he has great potential, my mentee disappointed me with his lack of effort and sense of urgency. During our meeting, he asked me mostly the same questions he asked during our last meeting eleven months ago. He took thorough notes from that meeting, but had made no progress toward following any of the crucial steps I suggested to propel his business forward. In fact, he had done absolutely nothing of major significance. He offered no valid excuses for his lack of progress, putting his head down and repeating, "Yeah. I have to get moving." Frustrated, I simply gave him the same information from before and admonished him to follow immediately the advice I gave him. I am afraid that my words went in one ear and out the other.

After our two-hour meeting, I began to think about what his poor follow-through and hesitation meant. To better understand, I recalled how I felt about pursing my entrepreneurial endeavors while in college and shortly after graduating. My sense of urgency to create a profitable business was almost an obsession. Some people would say it was indeed an obsession, as I was always running home to code and to add a feature to my website. I didn't have time for anything else except for doing the necessary tasks to move my business forward. School, a demanding girlfriend, and the desire to hang out with my friends were no obstacle for me. I made it happen regardless of the circumstances. I certainly wasn't going to wait around and do nothing. Even as I worked hard on growing my company, I felt like time was slipping away, like a competitor was just waiting for me to make a mistake.

The best entrepreneurs create environments of stressful urgency. Entrepreneurs know that start-ups rarely get anything done in a relaxed, take-your-time environment. For example, Steve Jobs, the cofounder of Apple, was notorious for pushing his team beyond its limits by setting seemingly unrealistic timelines. As a result, his company created products quicker than they had ever imagined was possible and thus gained a huge competitive advantage over rival companies like IBM.

Doctors and psychologists believe that stress caused by time constraints or urgency has an upside. In fact, they argue that we all need stress in our lives to perform certain tasks at a high level, ranging from avoiding a car accident to finishing a report for work. A recent MSNBC.com article explored the benefits of stress: "When the brain perceives physical or psychological stress, it starts pumping the chemicals cortisol, epinephrine (adrenaline) and norepinephrine into the body. Instantly, the heart beats faster, blood pressure increases, senses sharpen, a rise in blood glucose invigorates us and we're ready to rock." The article also quoted Janet DiPietro, a developmental psychologist at the Johns Hopkins Bloomberg School of Public Health: "When you have a deadline, when you have to perform, you want some stress to help you do your best."

If you lack the sense of urgency to grow your business, evaluate why you want to be in business. Perhaps you are not passionate about the business idea. Maybe your subconscious tells you that the idea isn't worth pursuing. Maybe the idea isn't yours and you feel no allegiance to it, or maybe you lack the self-discipline to be an entrepreneur. Whatever the reason, your lack of enthusiasm is not a good sign.

Before our meeting ended, my mentee gave me a clue as to why he called the meeting even if it seemed he hadn't been making progress. He revealed that he had to make money to support himself soon and that he had been offered a decent job that he doesn't necessarily want to take. I had a much better understanding of his circumstance and his sudden sense of urgency. It was telling. I concluded the meeting by reiterating that he should be working harder than ever to grow his company because time is running out. However, experience and entrepreneurial intuition tell me that he will end up getting a job working for someone else. He wasted too much valuable time.

6) Build a Company That Is Systems-Dependent, Not People-Dependent

Systems are the essential building blocks of every successful business.
—Ron Carroll, entrepreneur, business coach

As a computer science major in college matriculating with some of the brightest students from around the world, I quickly learned that my computer programming skills were not the most economical. I could get the job done, but not in the most efficient way. I would take one hundred lines of computer programming code to do something that my peers could do in ten. Such efficiency translates into faster programs and smaller-sized files. I eventually improved my programming skills because success in technologically related fields relies largely on the ability to implement efficient systems and methodologies.

The pioneer in creating systems that increase work efficiency was Henry Ford, founder of the Ford Motor Company. Ford created an assembly-line system that enabled him to mass-produce the Model T car. Before his introduction of the assembly line in 1913, a small team of specialists made cars, and the process was lengthy. Ford's methods, though, reduced the time from more than twelve hours to two hours and thirty minutes. His innovation put the car in the economic reach of an average family and improved productivity rates across many industries.

Not only did Ford's system boost productivity, but it also cut the need for the jack-of-all-trades. Instead, workers on the assembly line could be specialized, which also made them easier to replace. Before the assembly line, if an employee who built most of a car was out sick, productivity would slow down and the arduous process of building a car by hand would be much more difficult to continue.

I didn't understand the importance of building and implementing systems in business until my company had become too dependent on people. For instance, when I started my first popular website in college, I learned that a growing business that relied totally on me wasn't sustainable. I would eventually burn out and be unable to serve the growing number of users. And if, for some reason, I couldn't run the business, it wasn't clear who would do what to keep it going. I had to make a change. Consequently, I created a content management tool to expedite web updates and give me more time, but even that wasn't enough after a while. I was growing too fast and needed to bring on other people. The need for a clear system and way of doing things was obvious.

As a result of these growing pains, I learned to do two things when I begin a business venture: First, clearly separate and describe the roles in the business in written form. Second, use technology to map out and build systems that simplify and automate important tasks.

Even if you are a one-person show, take the time to delineate the roles and expectations that people in your business will play. Write a job description for crucial positions like CEO, CFO, vice president of sales, vice president of operations, and so on. You may be doing one, two, or all of these roles at the start, but this activity forces you to conceptualize how each role, not an individual person, relates to your business. As alluded to earlier, people come and go, but the functions needed to keep your business going do not.

Moreover, using technology, create process maps to visualize how you will execute different tasks. This step helps you determine where your processes can be improved and see where technology can make your processes more efficient. For example, my company uses several tools to help automate social media campaigns. Powerful tools like HootSuite enable users to manage several social media accounts through one interface, and its functionality automates messages. One person can do the work of tens or hundreds of people. This technology has made my company more efficient, saving valuable time and increasing revenues.

Being a start-up doesn't mean you have to operate haphazardly and without systems. While some degree of organizational chaos is unavoidable, you should still create, think through, and continually optimize your systems so that you are less dependent on people. Taking this step up front puts you further along the path to reaching your goals and allows you to know you're in the mode of building a company.

7) Ask for Help

Tell everyone what you want to do and someone will want
to help you do it.
—W. Clement Stone, businessman, philanthropist

When I arrived at Morehouse College, where I would spend four crucial years of my life, I had a huge chip on my shoulder. About a year before my arrival, Morehouse offered and I had accepted a full academic scholarship to study computer science. My scholarship was funded by NASA and was intended to groom outstanding math and science majors to work in the space program upon graduation. That summer before classes officially began in August, I took part in a mandatory, six-week orientation program for the thirty or so NASA scholars at Morehouse. We were the elite students, and we knew it. Along with high SAT scores and GPAs, we had extremely high opinions of ourselves. These opinions would change quickly.

What we thought would be an easy summer filled with new-found independence and fun became a summer of torture. During the program, we took college courses, including advanced calculus and advanced computer programming. Our calculus class was taught by a stern alumnus who was the stereotypical difficult professor. There was never a right answer. Even when a student offered a correct answer in class, the professor would ask us, "Is this answer correct?" Going to class was like having your fingernails pulled out one by one. Our computer science professor was equally intimidating. He had a different approach, though. He was a soft-spoken, jovial guy, but he would laugh at you and make fun of you if you gave a wrong answer. And he would often digress, talking about life in general. The worst thing about the summer classes was our grades. For example, in our calculus class, the best grade on the first quiz was a 55, I think. My grade was closer to my age. It wouldn't get much better. The material, pace, and pressure were too hard. The NASA Project Space Program knew exactly what it was doing. It broke us down and it humbled us.

As a result, we were all scared to death of college and studied harder than ever to prepare for the first day of real classes in August. Students who had never struggled academically were on the verge of a breakdown at the NASA program. There was mass panic, but everyone tried to play it cool. Some of us formed study groups and curtailed our social activities. Many of us questioned our ability and fortitude to survive and to make it through college. Some bailed before the six-week program was over.

This period was especially difficult for me. Through high school I rarely had to ask for help in my courses. If something gave me trouble, I would figure it out. Now I had to ask for help—and from peers—something I wasn't comfortable doing at all. I thought that this was a sign of weakness, and my reluctance to ask for help caused me to pay a high academic price.

I learned my lesson as a student thanks to NASA, and I vowed not to make the same mistake when I became a CEO in business. In fact, seconds after I came up with my first business idea as a sophomore, I asked for help. I contacted my good friend and fellow NASA scholar, Chris, to hear what he thought about my company's new name and domain name. Also, before I started another college business, I invited about five entrepreneurs to an evening meeting to discuss my business idea and to get their feedback and help. I made it a habit to ask for help from day one. Many of these same people continue to give me their guidance today, more than ten years later. The help I have asked for and received has been invaluable to my company's growth and my personal development. Before long, asking for help became natural. I just had to get rid of my ego.

When you start your business, lose the ego immediately. It's the main reason that entrepreneurs don't seek help. An overinflated ego even prevents those who ask for help from receiving it. Rarely do people want to help those who act as though they don't need it. And there's a difference between being confident and having an ego that's too big for your own good. Confidence attracts people; ego repels them.

One of the quickest ways to lead a life of mediocrity or utter failure is to think that you can accomplish a major task all by yourself. The self-made man or woman is a myth. Even the greatest business minds of our time had to ask for help. One of my favorite examples is that of Mark Zuckerberg, who asked his parents to help finance his young company, Thefacebook. His parents gave him $85,000 in the summer of 2004 to help buy servers for his growing business. This money, according to a lawsuit, was intended for his college tuition. It doesn't hurt to ask, right? Whether it's your oversized ego or your tendency to be introverted that's stopping you, go beyond your comfort zone and ask for help. Your business depends on it.

8) Business Comes First, Family Second

Good things happen when you get your priorities straight.
—Scott Caan, actor

I am almost 100 percent sure that the concept of putting business before family has caused me to lose some followers on Twitter, or at least it has given some of my followers a negative perception of me. Who in the world admits to putting their business before their family? To the average person, this notion is ludicrous and totally not politically correct.

When I first tweeted about how my business comes first and family second, I received the following comments: "You lost some friends on that one." "I disagree. I always put my family first." I cringed when I saw these and other comments pop up in my Twitter feed. I certainly don't like to invite controversy, but I think people who aren't die-hard entrepreneurs miss my point. I don't blame them necessarily, because I can't explain my reasoning within the 140 characters that Twitter allows. Ironically, I didn't receive any backlash from seasoned entrepreneurs. Something tells me they understood.

Some of the pushback on this comment came from people who work a normal job. The irony of their comments was overwhelming. Some said, "I always put family first." I doubt it. If they wanted to take off a year to take care of a sick parent and relied on the income of their job, they couldn't do it. They would get fired. They are beholden to the employer.

Why do top-performing entrepreneurs put their businesses first? I'll use an analogy to explain. When informing passengers of emergency procedures on airplanes, flight attendants always tell adult passengers traveling with a child to put on their oxygen mask first before they put one on a child. It's counterintuitive, but it makes sense when you think about it. Children depend on adult passengers to protect them because they cannot put on their own mask. If you do not follow this procedure, you could lose consciousness before giving a child a chance to live. This simple step saves lives. Similarly, business is a life-or-death situation. If you don't take care of your business first, everyone could eventually "die." As my father often says, quoting a Bible passage, if you don't work, you don't eat.

Likewise, I love how financial guru Suze Orman discourages parents from starting a college fund for their children if they don't have adequate savings. She admonishes them, saying, "Slow down! Your children will be better off if your finances are in order first."

Now that I've explained putting business first, let's take a step back. I don't follow this rule absolutely. Of course, there are some exceptions: I wouldn't miss a close family member's funeral, for example. However, if I am about to close a million-dollar deal and my son asks me to play catch that evening, my son will have to take a rain check. It's not cruel; it's common sense. Though he may be disappointed in the short term, he'll really appreciate the income later—perhaps in the form of receiving front-row seats at the Braves game right next to baseball legend Hank Aaron.

One of the biggest advantages of entrepreneurship is independence and flexibility to prioritize. If your business is doing well, you deserve to take more breaks and to spend quality time with family. If not, you should be hard at work, making sure that you can provide for your family and generations to come.

9) Do What's Most Important First

The key is not to prioritize what's on your schedule, but to schedule your priorities.
—Stephen Covey, best-selling author, *The Seven Habits of Highly Effective People*

When I began learning how to play golf a few years ago, it was much harder than I thought it would be. Of all the different mental and physical things needed to execute a good swing, I had the most difficulty keeping my head down through the swing. I almost always lifted my head before making contact with the ball and therefore took a bad swing. Sometimes I missed the ball altogether. It was so challenging because keeping my head down felt so unnatural. It was completely counterintuitive.

Likewise, doing the tasks that are most important in business is counterintuitive. Normally, these crucial tasks demand more time, energy, and focus than we care to give. Thus, we avoid them, doing those simpler tasks that really don't have a major impact on our business. Like a novice golfer who struggles with the basics, many entrepreneurs can't seem to master the habit of doing what's most valuable for their business. This basic discipline is the key to continued success as an entrepreneur.

If you are like most entrepreneurs, the lure of crossing something off your task list is too great to pass up. As you bask in the happiness of having crossed off another menial task, the more important tasks are pushed further down your to-do list and often forgotten. It's ironic how the most important items keep getting put off and therefore become, in reality, a low priority. We fool ourselves into believing that we are actually making significant progress by doing several little things.

On the contrary, veteran and smart entrepreneurs give priority to those tasks that are painful but which pay off in the end. They have the ability to ignore the fleeting satisfaction that may come from finishing small tasks. As a result, they seem to have the unique ability to accomplish so much more in a smaller time span. They don't have superpowers. Instead, they have super priorities and habits that make it easier to do what's most important.

A few simple tips can help you focus on the most important tasks that will take your business to new heights.

1. *Do important tasks first thing in the morning when you get up*. This is perhaps the most useful habit that has helped me become much more efficient. If I am working on a book, writing music, doing research, or producing computer code, my mind is freshest in the morning. Also, with fewer distractions in the morning, your focus is at its best.

2. *Change your environment*. Sometimes all you need to boost your productivity is a change in environment. If you work at home, steal away to a small park, or if you are in an office, go to a cafe. It's amazing how something so simple can improve your output. Some environments may subconsciously cause you to have more anxiety or stress than others. Identify and avoid them. Who knows? When you change your surroundings, maybe you'll receive an infusion of creativity like never before. It has happened to me.

3. *Disconnect from the real world*. Don't check your e-mail before or during work. Turn off the television and telephone. These interrupters cloud your focus. Research has shown that multitasking negatively affects your productivity. Also, the brain is most effective when it focuses on doing one thing.

4. *Take substantive breaks*. Do something that takes your mind completely off the task at hand. For example, I like to go for a run, go get the mail, or dance. Moving around helps me rejuvenate and gets my blood flowing. Whatever you do, don't take a break by staying at your desk or by staying in the same room where you work. Definitely change your scenery, and if you can, do a physical activity for at least five minutes.

Now that I have learned to keep my head down through my swing, my golf game has improved considerably. In fact, what was once uncomfortable and unnatural has become second-nature. Similarly, if you follow the preceding tips, your business game will improve, too. You will start to accomplish a lot more, and doing what's most important will be automatic.

10) Hire a Good Lawyer

A good business attorney will provide vital assistance in almost every aspect of your business.
—Cliff Ennico, author, *The Small Business Survival Guide*

If you've been in business long enough, sooner or later you will need sound legal advice from an attorney. Yes, you can use an Internet legal services firm, but you'll eventually need face-to-face counsel. Here are three common uses for legal services among start-ups and a few real-life examples of how an attorney helped my company.

First, *when you are ready to start your business, an attorney will recommend a legal entity that is best for you.* Do you set up a sole proprietorship, a C corporation, an S corporation, a limited liability company, or a limited liability partnership? Which is best?

When I started my company years ago, an attorney gave me wise advice. He suggested that I consider the long-term implications and flexibility of the legal entity I chose. He recommended that I select the entity that best fit my long-term vision for the company. A sole proprietorship, for instance, would not be the best option for a founder who plans to sell shares in the future. Of course, I could change classifications, but an extra cost is involved. Ideally, select the best option in the beginning and keep it.

Although you can find plenty of information online about different business classifications, discuss your specific situation with an attorney who can assess your needs and ultimately help you make the right decision.

Second, *an attorney helps you protect your intellectual property*

(*IP*). There is a good reason you cannot take The Coca-Cola Company's name and logo and use it to sell a beverage product—or any product for that matter. Not only is such behavior unscrupulous, it is also illegal. Specifically, it violates U.S. trademark law. In the same way that The Coca-Cola Company needs to protect its intellectual property, you want to protect yours. Intellectual property, defined generally as creations of the mind, includes mainly patents, copyrights, and trademarks.

Protecting my company's IP has saved me from costly litigation and frustration. Because of the popularity of my company's brands, we have had to deal with many impostors who try to capitalize on our success by stealing our IP. The perpetrators have ranged from publicly traded companies to careless individuals. For example, one company literally used our trademark to produce an event by the same exact name in the same city as our headquarters. My attorney promptly advised me to send the company a cease-and-desist letter, demanding that the company immediately stop using our trademark or it would risk litigation. The company complied with our request. Had we not the proper legal advice and proof of ownership of the trademark, we would have had much less recourse.

If you believe in the value of your products and services, protect your IP from the very start, no matter the cost. Many start-ups fail to protect their IP because of the relatively high cost. Cutting corners now costs more later. In particular, you could be forced to change your product's branding, restricted to sell in specific regions, or ordered to pay damages to someone suing you for abusing their own IP.

Third, *an attorney reviews the legal documents your company creates and receives from others to ensure that your interests are protected.* These documents may include contracts, agreements, and insurance policies.

As mentioned earlier, my attorney recently reviewed correspondence with companies that had infringed on our trademarks.

Her insight and guidance were crucial to a quick and favorable result in the matters.

By the way, many generic contracts can be found online for use, but be careful. These contracts may not provide you as much protection as you need. In fact, some of the contracts could do more harm than good. Generic contracts are sometimes a good start, but ultimately an attorney should review all contracts to be safe.

Attorneys often get a bad rap, I suppose from people who have lousy or no legal counsel during unfortunate circumstances. However, if you are prepared and proactive with your legal strategy, you will love your lawyer. Make sure that you protect the most important asset you have, your company, with adequate legal services from an attorney.

11) The Business Plan Is Overrated

No business plan survives first contact with a customer.
—Steve Blank, Silicon Valley–based retired serial entrepreneur

After conjuring up a brilliant business idea, I would immediately start writing a business plan. Like a skilled magician, I could make a marvelous business plan appear before your eyes in just a few days. It would be complete with colorful graphs, in-depth market research, and detailed financials. The plan would be ready to execute. And I was sure it had as many pages as possible. Why? I once heard an investor say that he only considers investing in companies with plans that make a thump when you drop them on a table. After years of practical business experience, I realized that I didn't make a good magician and I was only fooling myself. Now I know better.

Experience has taught me that when I get a new business idea, working on the business plan is one of the last things to do. The three crucial steps I follow before even thinking of writing a business plan will work for you, too. First, *examine the competitive landscape to see what companies are already there.* What do they do poorly? What can you do differently to create a competitive advantage? Second, *discuss the idea with potential customers*, asking basic questions that determine how much they would value your product or service, which is perhaps the most important preliminary step to writing the business plan. Third, *develop a sketch or basic prototype of the product.* If it's a service, map out vital steps and describe customer experiences.

By the way, when you are finally ready to write the business plan, make sure that you find professional help in areas that aren't your expertise. If you don't understand how to project cash flow for the next five years, don't attempt it. Likewise, if you don't know anything about marketing, which is likely the most important part of your plan, you shouldn't be writing that section. A business plan should be a collaboration, not a solo endeavor. As a well-respected serial entrepreneur once told me, investors are skeptical of any business plan written by one person.

Even the academic world, known for resisting change, is reassessing the importance of the business plan. Candida Brush, chair of the entrepreneurship division and director of the Arthur M. Blank Center for Entrepreneurship at Babson College in Wellesley, Massachusetts, put it best in a recent interview with *Entrepreneur* magazine:

> Students come in here saying they want to write a business plan, but that's the last thing they need to do. The only way to get to a point where you have a truly entrepreneurial idea is to use a creative approach. Observe. Reflect. Do mini experiments, as opposed to sitting in the library reading case studies. . . . And for us, even that plan is about the process, not creating a 50-page action plan. If you get married to a bad idea, a business plan means nothing.

Babson students are encouraged to do three feasibility studies before moving forward with an idea or writing a business plan. The studies are similar to the steps I mentioned above. More universities and entrepreneurs should adopt this approach.

In short, too much emphasis is still placed on writing a business plan when you have an idea. There is an epidemic of "Franken-plans," business plans that are a sloppy amalgamation of various business plans or templates; having the document itself seems more important than the quality of the actual plan. Instead of rushing to finish the document, make sure you take the crucial preliminary steps before you begin writing. If done thoroughly, these steps make your business plan stronger and greatly improve your chances of success and funding.

12) Require Criticism and Disagreement in Your Company

Honest disagreement is often a good sign of progress.
—Mahatma Gandhi, Indian nationalism leader, social activist

Michael Jordan is the laughingstock of the National Basketball Association (NBA). Jordan—who dominated the NBA for years, won six championships with the Chicago Bulls, was crowned Most Valuable Player of the league five times, and still continues to be one of the most recognized sports figures in the world—is shooting air balls, as it were. As owner of the Charlotte Bobcats, he has been unable to translate his success on the court into success in the front office. During the 2011–2012 NBA season, his Bobcats had the worst winning percentage in NBA history. They reached their nadir. As their season ended in total shame, the players and owners prepared for a different game during the off-season: the blame game.

While the heated debate continues about what's needed to save this franchise from complete collapse, most people already agree that the lack of Jordan's leadership is a major problem. Charles Barkley, a former NBA player turned commentator, has chided his friend in public, implying that Jordan is an aloof owner who lacks management ability and has no interest in running a winning team. Many of Jordan's closest confidants agree that the Bobcats' leadership must be changed. Furthermore, they point to a culture of acquiescence that prevents the franchise from moving forward. In other words, Jordan is surrounded by yes-men minions who are afraid to tell him what he needs to hear in order to improve the team. This defeating culture can shoot down a business as easily as a basketball franchise.

When my company was young I committed the mistake of creating a culture in which everyone agreed with me. I only accepted individuals on my team who thought like me or who took orders happily. Also, in the same way that Jordan intimidates members of the Bobcats organization, I apparently had the same effect. Like Jordan, I was the superstar with a history of success. No one was willing to challenge me or my ideas to take the company to a higher level. I was somewhat aware of this internal culture, but I didn't think it was harmful. Moreover, I wasn't mature or confident enough to actively seek out dissenting opinions. As a result, my company didn't reach its full potential. A culture that encouraged frequent criticism and disagreement could have led to that kind of success.

Now I actively seek people who will ruffle my feathers by criticizing my ideas. When possible, I make these critics a part of my team. Otherwise, I keep them close by for consultation. If I find people who can really get under my skin and make me question my way of thinking, I am especially motivated. I work harder because I want to prove them wrong—either by strengthening my case or by finding a better way. If my ideas aren't working, I often adopt their suggestions. Through this process, my company is stronger.

My latest venture, a data analytics company, has benefited tremendously from a culture in which ideas are challenged routinely. For instance, going against the yes-man faction at the company, we opted to use new Agile methods to create our product. Consequently, product development is faster and leaner.

Going from celebrated champion to ridiculed loser is not what Jordan had in mind when he decided to assume ownership of the Charlotte Bobcats. However, he may be out of his league, and it's largely his fault. He now understands, like so many other business leaders, that he must employ people who tell him when he is headed in the wrong direction. Otherwise, his odds of turning around his franchise are next to nil.

Take a lesson from Michael Jordan's ownership woes and my less exciting anecdotes. Surround yourself with honest people who tell you the good, the bad, and the ugly. If you don't, you may become the laughingstock of your industry, too.

So much for the theme of the classic Gatorade commercial that featured Jordan: "I wanna be like Mike!"

13) Fire Your Worst Customers

Successful organizations (and I include churches and political parties on the list) fire the 1 percent of their constituents that cause 95 percent of the pain.
—Seth Godin, entrepreneur, author

When most entrepreneurs start their business, they take every customer they can get. This approach reminds me of my obsession with scoring in my elementary school basketball games. As an adolescent benchwarmer with almost no playing time, I would rush to shoot once I finally received the opportunity to play. The more shots I took, the better my chances of scoring and declaring success. The overall score and team strategy didn't matter. I rarely scored, and I looked like a headless chicken as I took the most ridiculous and inelegant shots. I was so focused on getting and shooting the ball that I once made a basket for the opposing team while on defense. Similarly, entrepreneurs often do more damage to themselves and their team by making haphazard attempts to score every potential customer.

Every veteran entrepreneur has scored for the other team, so to speak. In other words, we have all had customers who take advantage of us, and we allow them to do so. In some cases, this situation can be perfectly fine, but it is not ideal when your business loses money. Frequently, we only realize at the point of no return that the unfavorable situation in which we find ourselves could have been avoided; we could have passed on the customer altogether.

Making the decision to pass on a customer is especially difficult for young or new entrepreneurs who are hungry for business and revenues. However, choosing bad customers can cause a lot of frustration, drain resources, damage your reputation, and eventually put you out of business.

To help you decide what customers are worth your time, consider four important signs which indicate that you should not take a client and gracefully move on from the relationship. These signs apply especially to entrepreneurs who run a service-oriented or consulting business.

1. *Be skeptical of a client who seems not to know what is needed or who constantly makes changes.* For example, if you have a web or graphic design company, explain clearly your creative process and the time needed for the project. Quantify all expectations. Some designers, for instance, agree to do three prototypes. Afterward, the client must choose from those three prototypes. Avoid at all costs a situation in which you are designing or creating indefinitely, only to have the client make a choice on the tenth iteration. Also, a client should be comfortable with your capabilities and what to expect from you. Find out from new clients what attracted them to your work. Show your portfolio.

2. *Be careful if a client is not willing to pay an hourly rate or a piece rate of some kind.* Agreeing to a fixed cost for your work is not bad per se. However, it's not so great if you end up doing more

work than you anticipated. Many clients encourage you to lower your cost to lock in a good rate. In a gesture of good faith, sometimes the client will pay you all the money up front. That way, you are beholden to the client until it receives a deliverable it likes. These types of arrangements can be especially stressful and strain a relationship to the point of litigation.

3. *Avoid any client who hesitates to sign a well-written agreement.* This is a true test of whether a client is worth your time and effort. An agreement or contract protects both parties and outlines expectations. Without a comprehensive agreement you have no way to protect your interests, assess the progress of the work you have done, and verify the deliverable.

4. *Take heed of any less than good feelings you have about a potential client.* I have learned to accept my business intuition, and I would say that 80 percent of the time it leads me to make better decisions about a potential client's value.

I recently received a request for my company's services from a former client who cost me a lot more money than I made. In fact, the experience of working with the company was terrible. As a result, I respectfully rejected the overture and recommended another company. I learned the hard way the first time and decided that I would do all I could to avoid the agony next time. Don't be afraid to fire a client. Just because some customers want you doesn't mean you need them.

14) Make Money While Doing Nothing

$1,000,000 in the bank isn't the fantasy. The fantasy is the lifestyle of complete freedom it supposedly allows.
—Timothy Ferriss, author, *The 4-Hour Workweek*

In the 1200s, the Third Council of the Lateran, a group of Christian bishops, declared that anyone who charged and accepted interest on a loan would be denied sacraments and Christian burial. Usury was eventually determined a heresy and outlawed, relegating the practice to Jews, whose holy law, the Torah, allowed them to loan to non-Jews. Christian leaders and their followers strongly believed that charging interest on a loan was an abomination to God. Their reasoning was based on the Holy Bible and the interpretation of relevant passages by contemporary scholars. Many reasons were given, but one is especially noteworthy: They believed that labor without the expenditure of energy was a sin.

Times have certainly changed, but disdain for those who gain wealth from inheriting money, charging interest, or making effortless deals still manifests itself—whether through Occupy Wall Street protests or petty gossip. The average person, especially one who labors physically, abhors the idea of people amassing wealth by doing nothing. It goes against the good ol' Protestant work ethic on which the United States was built. The idea, often fueled by intense jealousy, makes many people quite uncomfortable.

I never thought I would be on the receiving end of such aversion and jealousy. Recently, during the planning of an extended family vacation, a disgruntled family member commented, "I can't go on vacation that long! Everybody can't be like Kevin." When I heard this, I was shocked. Apparently, because my income doesn't depend on me working in the traditional sense, I was the object of ridicule. I kept quiet. Dealing with such things is a small price to pay. It's certainly not as bad as actually having to work for income or being denied a proper burial.

The reactions of people throughout history and in my own experience are understandable. Entrepreneurs who have figured out how to make money while doing nothing have reached the upper echelon of entrepreneurship. These overachievers have mastered the strategies that allow them to reach this level, which is where all of us want to be, and it is a major accomplishment. Having a profitable business that can run well without you is true freedom.

But what is meant by "doing nothing"? In my opinion, the term isn't so absolute. For simplicity, I'll use the term popularized by a best-selling book of the same name. If your business can run while you enjoy *The 4-Hour Workweek* or less, then you fall into the doing-nothing category. By the way, the work that goes into setting up a business that runs without its founder is often overlooked. "Doing nothing" disregards the work the entrepreneur put in beforehand. For example, it took me years of trial and error and diligent work to master the concepts needed to be free.

So what strategies can carry you to this high level of entrepreneurship? In a nutshell, the strategies—already covered in this book—are *removing yourself from your business, building systems that are not people-dependent, automating activities using technology,* and *outsourcing to the right partners.* These suggestions certainly aren't comprehensive, and you don't have to employ all of them in any order, but they provide a general idea of the type of thinking that will get you to independence. I expand on these concepts in other parts of this book.

Drawing profits from one business while starting the next is a great feeling. That's the life of an entrepreneur's entrepreneur. In fact, as I write this, PayPal sent me a Notification of Payment Received for one of my businesses. How apropos!

I failed to mention something earlier. I have a very different definition of working. Instead of being stuck in an office, I would much prefer that my workday be like a recent excursion with a client. We went on a safari in Nairobi, Kenya, and walked the beach with camels in Mombasa, Kenya. During the trip, I was able to check my financial dashboards every now and then on my mobile. That's my idea of work.

15) Outsourcing Makes Sense

If you deprive yourself of outsourcing and your competitors do not, you're putting yourself out of business.
—Lee Kaun Yew, former prime minister, Singapore

In at least two episodes of *Shark Tank*, the popular ABC show in which entrepreneurs get a chance to pitch their business idea to and receive funding from investors, some stubborn business owners refused to manufacture their products where costs were lowest for the desired quality. Each entrepreneur had a solid business with customers and significant revenues, but neither company was profitable, largely because production costs were so high. The sharks, who immediately realized the problem, suggested that the entrepreneurs produce their goods in China, where costs would be much cheaper and thus profits much higher. However, both owners were adamant about continuing to manufacture in the United States and creating jobs at home, an admirable but naïve decision that would likely shut them down altogether. Ironically, while trying to create more jobs in the country they love, they would likely add to the high unemployment rate. The investors, who were originally excited about the businesses, ultimately lost interest because of the owners' reluctance to outsource.

The episodes were quite emotional. In fact, one of the owners was on the verge of tears because he so strongly believed in what he was doing for his country. His conviction prevented him from taking the sharks' advice. In a final attempt to make a deal, a shark tried to get one of the owners to understand that he could have more of an impact on his community plagued by high unemployment if his business were successful. The shark's efforts were futile. Though rattled, the owner stood pat, realizing that he could be making the biggest mistake of his life. As a frustrated television viewer and business owner, I certainly thought he was.

Since our economy has taken a turn for the worse, "outsourcing" has become a dirty word, tantamount to "traitor" or "anti-American." What true American wouldn't want to create jobs here at home, right? The United States, where outsourcing was once a popular trend and great for business, suddenly threw globalism by the wayside and adopted an ideology of isolationism. Television sitcoms like *Outsourced*, in which an American corporation outsources its call center to India, don't help the matter. In an uncommon display of political harmony, the Republican and Democratic Parties agree that keeping jobs in America is a top priority to grow our economy and to get it back to more prosperous times. However, ignoring politics and using common sense, the campaign against outsourcing does more harm than good when it comes to economic development.

Quite simply, the benefits of outsourcing outweigh any negatives as its opponents describe them. Besides, you must do what's best for your business. Whether you're sending work to a contractor in Singapore or a vendor in South Carolina, outsourcing is good for business. Any functionality that is not core to your business should be outsourced at the best cost and quality. In the majority of cases, trying on your own to produce everything that your business needs is unrealistic and highly inefficient. If you have believed the negative hype about outsourcing, quickly disabuse yourself of it and implement the process into your business strategy. If you're subscribing to the propaganda and refusing to even consider outsourcing, your competitors are meanwhile outsourcing and working hard to put you out of business. You don't need to be a high-profile shark to understand this reality.

16) Move On Fast from a Bad Business Idea

Nothing is more dangerous than an idea when it is the only
one you have.
—Emile Chartier, French philosopher, journalist

"My company is headed for sure failure, and I think the best thing to do is to shut it down before things get worse." How many times have you heard such a candid assessment of a business by its founder? If you are like me, it's probably not often. During my twelve years of being in business and in associated professional circles, I can count on one hand the number of times an entrepreneur has told me that a company is doing poorly or is destined to crash and burn.

Why is that? Entrepreneurs are naturally tenacious, and expectedly so. They never give up; they stick with an idea until the death. We have all heard a miracle story or two that involves a founder who overcame great odds. Pandora, a company that Tim Westergren founded and that took ten years to turn a profit, comes to mind. It's quite an inspiring story of patience and persistence, but far from the norm.

Rarely is the negative side of entrepreneurial tenacity discussed, but I have witnessed so many entrepreneurs hold on to a bad idea far too long. They refuse to acknowledge that things are going south or have no promise, and they go down with the sinking ship. For instance, a good friend of mine finally threw in the towel on his men's marriage magazine. He stuck with it for almost an entire decade. I commend his determination, but I am happy he has moved on. It was like he kept trying to make a bad marriage work (pun intended). A smart guy, he would have been better off devoting his time to other ideas.

This problem is common among novice entrepreneurs. They tend to think that the idea they have is the only good one they've got, demanding an all-or-nothing response with no retreat possible.

However, serial entrepreneurs and those who have built massive amounts of wealth in business rarely make this mistake. Through their experience, they have learned how to determine whether to stay with an idea and for how long. Their previous success enables them to admit their failures freely and move on to the next opportunity.

Regardless of your business experience, you want to avoid the untamed-tenacity syndrome. Unfortunately, no definitive list of signs lets you know if you should abandon your idea. One reason is that signs can be specific to an industry.

For example, I would have told my friend with the magazine to listen closely to Marc Andreessen, cofounder of Netscape and venture capitalist, in a recent television interview. I paraphrase: "Publications should cut their losses by shutting down their presses and moving to the digital realm. Print is dead. Advertising dollars in print are drying up for that medium. Therefore, now is not the ideal time to start a print publication." Your circumstance may be different. Perhaps your breakeven point is too far down the road based on industry metrics, or your market is too small to be profitable. As alluded to in the magazine scenario, you must find the oracles and special metrics in your industry to make sure you are on track.

Reiterating Chartier's statement at the beginning of this section, an entrepreneur with a single idea can be catastrophic. Don't let a bad idea derail your plans for greatness. If it isn't working, move on or adjust quickly.

17) A Bad Economy Is a Great Opportunity

---

*A pessimist sees the difficulty in every opportunity; an optimist
sees the opportunity in every difficulty.*
—Winston Churchill, prime minister, United Kingdom
(1940–45, 1951–55)

Times were good. No, they were great. My company had just
passed six figures in revenue, and it was headed to break the sev-
en-figure mark. My team grew to almost twenty people, all of
whom were passionate about the business and exceeded my expectations. Various local and national publications were calling me to
secure an interview so that they could highlight me, a young entrepreneur with great potential. I even received a call from a financial
representative with Northwestern Mutual who saw me featured in a
magazine and thought I would be a great client. We met, and he
handed me a three-ring leather binder with a detailed plan that
would enable me to retire comfortably by age forty. I was barely in
my twenties.

Fast-forward a few years to now. The glory days are long gone.
As President Barack Obama puts it, we continue to face the worst
economic times since the Great Depression. Since 2008, my company revenues have dropped. Sometimes it feels like the challenging financial times of our start-up days. The team no longer con-
sists of twenty people, and some of our best and brightest have
moved on to other ventures. If I appear in any publication or on
television, it's rarely to showcase my success. Instead, it's more
likely to give advice on how to stay afloat during this economic
maelstrom. My financial plan needs adjustment. Retiring by age
forty is not going to happen. Despite the gloom, I know that the
glory days will be back soon. History and experience tell me so.

Many of the biggest companies in history—and smaller ones,
too—thrived during a bad economy. For example, Microsoft,
founded by Bill Gates and Paul Allen, was started during a reces-

sion in 1975. During that time, unemployment was high and gas prices were through the roof due to OPEC's decision to increase prices drastically. A few other companies founded during difficult economic times are Disney, IBM, and General Motors. Similarly, many companies already in existence have made comebacks during challenging financial periods. Perhaps the most familiar and recent example is Apple, which began its resurgence in 2001 during the dotcom bust and the effects of the September 11, 2001, tragedy.

As I reflect on companies that weathered the storm, I remember that I started my company in 2000 during the time of the dotcom bust and brief recession. In fact, I vividly remember major news media reporting on the huge number of unemployed college graduates. The signs of an impending, severe recession were multiplying, especially after the 9/11 attacks. Despite the bad signs, I was fortunate that my youth and temerity enabled me to see the world through a positive lens. I knew that hard work would pay off, no matter what the circumstances. It certainly did.

In short, entrepreneurs do not allow a bad economy to hold them back from accomplishing their goals. Ironically, poor economic conditions often have the opposite effect; they motivate entrepreneurs more and propel them to success even faster. Times are not so great as I write, but entrepreneurs ignore the zeitgeist and create positive circumstances. They roll up their sleeves and get to work, anticipating the next growth period. That's where you want to be: ready to grab the bull by its horns and ride.

18) Adopt Technology Early

Any new technology tends to go through a 25-year adoption cycle.
—Marc Andreessen, cofounder, Netscape; venture capitalist

Growing up in Boston around some of the sharpest and creative minds, I was quite fortunate. Advanced computer technology was woven into the fabric of everyday life. In a way, being a nerd was cool, I guess because there were so many of us.

My adolescent best friend, who eventually attended Massachusetts Institute of Technology, and I built an interactive website on an intranet for a class presentation in tenth grade back in 1994. While we were in high school, his father was a research scientist for the Bates Linear Accelerator Center (nuclear physics) for MIT, so the computer science labs on MIT's campus were sometimes our stomping grounds. I remember the halcyon days of hacking on purple-accented, Sun Microsystems Ultra workstations while leaning back in our swivel chairs that had ATHENA painted in big white letters on the back.

Likewise, I was exposed in my youth to projects that the average person can only dream about or read about in science fiction novels. For example, we would visit places like MITRE Corporation, an organization that did extensive research for the Department of Defense and the Federal Aviation Administration. The company also conducted research to explore new technologies. As an adolescent, I vividly remember speaking to a scientist who developed the *real* version of the toy Nintendo Power Glove. He mentioned that the project cost hundreds of thousands of dollars. We also saw other innovations with lasers and biometrics that are just reaching the commercial market today.

I mention all of this because my background gives me tremendous perspective on how innovations eventually reach the commercial market. Most of us who are members of the digerati know that the Internet is not new, for instance. In fact, it was around in its primitive forms as early as 1958. My first encounter with the Internet was through Prodigy in 1990, when I religiously wrote my pen pal, Rachel, in San Francisco via electronic mail. Remember that Velcro was adopted by NASA in the late 1950s for space travel and eventually found widespread practical use here on earth. Technological innovation takes, in many cases, decades to reach the consumer market. Nowadays, that process is often condensed to just a few years.

Researching the backgrounds of many of the most successful tech entrepreneurs reveals a common thread. Like me, they were exposed to new and exclusive technologies at an early point, allowing them to master these technologies and adopt them for eventual commercial use. For example, cofounder of Apple Steve Jobs infiltrated Xerox's PARC and "borrowed" the graphical user interface. Similarly, Reed Hastings, founder of Netflix, was exposed to early DVD technology that would inspire his business idea, and so on. The media glorification of so many successful tech entrepreneurs would lead you to believe that their achievements are the result of pure genius. However, we know better. These entrepreneurs were often exposed early to technologies that gave context to and inspired their genius.

What does all of this mean for you? Not only are entrepreneurs early adopters, but they also explore technologies way before they are even introduced to the general public for consumption. Thus, find every opportunity to learn about what technology is the next big thing. This practice pays tremendous dividends.

19) Ignorance Can Be Bliss

To succeed in life, you need two things: ignorance and confidence.
—Mark Twain, author, humorist

Pete Kight has a success story that is simply amazing. The company he founded, CheckFree, was acquired in 2007 by Fiserve for approximately $4.4 billion in cash. In many ways, his story sounds like other millionaire success stories that include dropping out of school, being ridiculed for pursuing a big idea, receiving rejection after rejection from prospective customers, having little money, and so on. But one aspect of his story is truly inspiring, and it serves as a profound lesson in entrepreneurship.

I was fortunate to hear Pete relate his fascinating accomplishments in person and in his own words just a few months before his company was acquired. He began telling his story before a crowd of students, entrepreneurs, and dignitaries: "I didn't do well in school. In fact, I dedicated most of my time and energy to sports. I was a decathlete. After getting injured and becoming frustrated with college, I dropped out. . . ." His delivery was unimpressive, marked by monotony and an awkward cadence, but everyone was still riveted. The nontraditional path he took to success held everyone's attention. He didn't need the swagger or panache of a Donald Trump or the enlightenment of a Warren Buffett.

Pete finished his story, talking about how he became a manager of health clubs and began exploring the idea of deducting monthly health-club payments from checking accounts. He was frustrated with a payment system that required high-pressure sales and a lot of manual work to collect payments. Convinced by his vision to change the financial industry, Pete eventually hired a computer programmer and operated his new electronic bill payment business out of his grandmother's basement in Ohio.

The most compelling part of Pete's speech was his admission that he knew nothing about computer software. In fact, he emphasized this fact. He commented that he didn't believe he would be as successful as he was in business if he knew how to program computers. Put another way, his ignorance about computers enabled him to focus on the more important aspects of growing his business. What a profound insight, considering that many of the millionaire or billionaire stories we hear come from individuals whose success largely depended on their technical talents and knowledge of their particular industry.

What do a majority of the top-twenty richest Americans have in common? They worked in the industry that they would eventually dominate. Bill Gates was a computer programmer; Warren Buffett was a trader; Larry Ellison studied computer design; George Soros was a trader; Jeff Bezos studied computer science; Mark Zuckerberg studied computer science as well. I could keep going down the *Forbes* 400 list, but some wealthy individuals have indeed broken the mold and challenged the assumption that you have to be highly familiar with the industry in which you plan to compete. Pete Kight is one of them. He came from neither a financial services background nor a computer programming background. As one investor who turned him down said, he was "a broken-down ex-jock." His achievements are that much more impressive.

What is my point? The data indicate that in order to be a wealthy individual or successful entrepreneur, you should probably be an expert in or knowledgeable of the industry you strive to dominate, although there are exceptions to that rule. Look at individuals like Pete Kight, founder of CheckFree; Sara Blakely, founder of Spanx; and Kevin Plank, founder of Under Armour. Conceiving of an idea that puts you outside of your area of expertise or comfort zone does not equal failure. Perhaps your outside perspective enables you to see things in a fresh way, seizing dormant opportunities. As Pete Kight proves, your ignorance could actually be your biggest advantage and account for your ultimate success.

20) Adapt to Change Quickly

Change before you have to.
—Jack Welch, former CEO, General Electric

The average lifespan of a Fortune 500 company is getting shorter and shorter, largely because of the ascendancy of disruptive technologies and companies. Small and nimble start-ups are often overlooked by big corporations and now have the ability with little resources to topple billion-dollar companies.

Substantive data show the increased attrition rate of big companies. An analysis of the major stock market indexes over the past few decades reveals that companies have shorter runs. For example, only a fraction of the companies listed on the Dow Jones Industrial Average in the 1980s remain on the list. What does this mean? Many things, but a closer look at the index's rejects sheds light on why companies were removed: Many of the companies vanished for failing to adapt to changing times and evolving with customer demands. Thus, it's safe to say that companies that do not embrace change and reinvent themselves are headed out of business fast.

Change is inevitable, but it is not easy. One of my favorite speakers and authors, Don Hutson, said this about change: "Change happens when the pain to stay the same exceeds the pain to change." Although Hutson was speaking to a group of individuals interested in improving themselves, the same principle applies to business. A business that doesn't change or reinvent itself periodically will experience the pain of bankruptcy. At that grim point, change is the only option.

Companies that have reached a degree of success are most likely to resist change and to stretch their pain threshold. If something is not broken, don't try to fix it, right? Wrong. There are countless examples of large companies that dominated the market for long periods, but now are struggling just to stay alive. A prime example

59

is Sears Roebuck and Co., which dominated the retail market for decades. Now it struggles to turn a profit. Sears rested on its laurels and missed opportunities to conquer the new business frontier in the 1990s: e-commerce. To Sears's great misfortune, competitors like Amazon.com and Walmart aggressively pursued the retail market and are now winning big.

The question then becomes: How do you manage and cope with change, especially as times and technology move so fast? Each of my companies has faced the challenge of staying relevant and keeping up with the times. As a result, I have a healthy sense of paranoia. I now use a basic strategy that minimizes the risk of my companies becoming complacent and unwilling to change. I conduct each company as if the way we do business is going to be obsolete in one to two years. To anticipate where the market is going and where we should invest, we do a bimonthly review and a report of all our systems and processes. The review allows us to identify and adapt to potential disruptions like new technology and competition.

For example, division heads provide a review and a report of how we can improve our products and services even if they are selling well. We also scan the competitive landscape to find any innovations that are threatening. In addition, we identify new technologies and resources that help us to stay ahead of the change curve. A recent company review, for instance, revealed how we can use Pinterest, a social media platform that became popular in 2012, to target new segments in our marketing campaigns that normally would be overlooked. We know from experience that the value of using such platforms is greater if you use them early. Waiting puts you at a huge disadvantage. This review and report process is one of the simplest ways to proactively seek change and to reinvent the way you do business, preventing you from becoming complacent and more vulnerable to obsolescence.

A business that ignores change is a business that welcomes its own extermination. The products or services you offer today won't keep you in business tomorrow. The very nature of business includes changing to meet customers' demands in a better way. If you have no strategy to proactively deal with change in your business, save yourself from a slow death and just shut down shop now.

21) Technology Is an Opportunity, Not a Threat

Technology has always been important, but we are standing on the precipice of an inflection point in human history. Technology is reaching what I call the knee of the curve, a point in time which its exponential growth is taking off at a nearly vertical slope. . . . The pace of progress is itself accelerating.
—Ray Kurzweil, author, *The Singularity Is Near*

The most challenging thing to do in business is to stay in business. According to the U.S. Department of Commerce, "Seven out of 10 new employer firms survive at least 2 years, half at least 5 years, a third at least 10 years, and a quarter stay in business 15 years or more." Evidently, as time increases, the odds of your company surviving decrease.

Time seems to be the common dooming factor for thousands of businesses, but a much more devastating agent is at work here, especially nowadays. That agent is technology. At a recent technology conference in Atlanta, Carlos Dominguez, senior vice president at Cisco, discussed how things that used to take a long time now happen quickly and effortlessly. One of his examples showcased the power of social media and its ability to spread information at unprecedented speeds. He related a story of how he used Twitter to avoid an immediate travel disaster in Mexico. He ended the series, declaring, "Times are exponential." I couldn't agree more. Technological innovation, whether rapid progress in computer science or nanotechnology, is seemingly causing the condensation of time. It is also driving many people out of business.

As an entrepreneur, you must be well aware of technology's power to alter your business. On the one hand, ignoring technology can mean your quick demise. On the other hand, if you adopt it early, it can catapult your business to tremendous growth. One way to stay on top of technological innovation is to implement strategies that promote and reward forward thinking in your company.

In his excellent book *Jump the Curve*, futurist Jack Uldrich discusses strategies to survive what he calls an "exponential economy," an economy driven by technological innovation. With compelling cases and commonsense analogies, he urges readers to stay ahead of the curve, referring to the curve on an exponential graph. One of his most convincing strategies is to think rationally about the implications of future-generation technology. To illustrate his point, he uses the case of Reed Hastings, founder of Netflix. Hastings, a former Peace Corps volunteer, realized after seeing DVD technology in 1996 that data storage would make huge advances. (It certainly did.) As a result, Hastings founded Netflix in 1999 and has grown his company to become a billion-dollar behemoth. Netflix continues to be an industry leader in the video/home rental market. Uldrich would say that Hastings was able to "jump the curve."

Likewise, I attribute my early entrepreneurial success to being able to see into the technological future and anticipating consumer demands that I could meet using new technologies. Realizing that publications and individuals had no simple tool to publish their content online, I created a web-based content management system called OmniPublisher. Users didn't have to know HTML, CSS, PHP, JavaScript, or any other computer programming language to use the software. They only needed to be comfortable with navigating a web browser in order to publish their own content online. As bandwidth capacity increased and Internet usage surged, OmniPublisher grew in popularity.

In 1977 Ken Olson, president and founder of Digital Equipment Corp. (DEC), proclaimed, "There is no reason anyone would want a computer in their home." His comment denounced the latest technological developments and favored his company's main product, business mainframe computers. Meanwhile—that same year, in fact—a burgeoning company called Apple was founded on the idea that everyone would have a personal computer someday. We all know how this story ends. In December 1980 Apple went public, propelled by the incredible sales of the Apple I.

There are countless stories of people resisting technological innovations and getting it wrong. These people claim that Facebook is spooky; Twitter is a waste of time; and Pinterest . . . what is that? These skeptics are the progeny of Ken Olson. Sooner or later, they, too, will be out of business. Don't let that happen to you.

22) Always Follow Up

Success comes from taking the initiative and following up.
—Anthony Robbins, author, professional speaker

A few months ago I had lunch with a good friend and mentor who is a member of one of the largest and most successful angel investor organizations in the United States. We meet from time to time to share stories, ideas, and opportunities.

Our lunch took place shortly after one of his organization's meetings, in which two entrepreneurs gave a brief presentation about their business and asked for investment capital. Members of the angel organization then discussed whether to advance the companies to the due-diligence phase required before committing any money. One company, a green company, had a compelling value proposition that I thought was worth funding.

I have been to several of these meetings, and no matter how many I attend, the experience never grows old or loses excitement. This is the big leagues, where big companies are made. Entrepreneurs who have reached this point have worked hard and fought for the opportunity to present before the angels. Despite receiving thousands of applications, the angels accept only a few companies to present before the body. For this reason, I was shocked to hear what my friend shared with me about one particular company that totally blew the opportunity.

A company that impressed the angels with a top-notch presentation and innovative product basically disappeared during the due-diligence process. The head of the committee assigned to carry out the due diligence never heard back from the company's CEO during the final stages of the process. The angels felt jaded. Their chairman even made several personal calls to the CEO, but he was nowhere to be found. Ironically, there were no hiccups during the due-diligence process. The company's request for funds was pretty much guaranteed. After several attempts to find the missing CEO, the angels gave up. At this point, they weren't so sure about investing in a person who doesn't have the decency to follow up anyway.

Apparently, the foibles that I thought were limited to novice business owners or CEOs of young start-ups were also common among more established companies. I couldn't believe it. In the back of my mind, I was thinking, *Give me a million dollars for my company, and I will pick up the phone so fast you will wonder if the phone even rang!* I don't know why the CEO disappeared, but there is no reason to leave such influential people—or anybody for that matter—hanging that way. Regardless of the circumstances, he should have let the angel group know. At the very least, it's common courtesy.

This classic case of an entrepreneur failing to follow up is a simple mistake that can have devastating consequences. It's a simple fact: Those who master the art of following up are more successful than those who do not, yet so many entrepreneurs overlook and underestimate this simple rule. Why?

1. *Fear of rejection causes many entrepreneurs to fail to follow up.* Learning how to deal with rejection years ago was especially difficult for me, as a young and somewhat antisocial computer programmer. Having to sell my ideas to others was frightening—

and quite frankly it still is sometimes. The only rejection I knew when I started my company was a compiler telling me that my program wouldn't run. (Don't worry if you didn't understand the last sentence. It's just computer talk.) No one likes being rejected, but you must get over this fear. I often interpret a no as meaning "not right now." I have learned more about my products and services from people telling me no than from people telling me yes. When you follow up with people, especially during a sales call or a negotiation, do it with complete confidence. If you receive a no, ask open-ended questions to learn why the situation didn't turn out the way you wanted. For example, if someone doesn't want to buy your product, ask, "What was the determining factor in your decision?" Turn a negative into a positive.

2. *Entrepreneurs lack the dedication and energy to follow up.* Following up takes concerted effort and planning. I never thought something could be so exhaustive. Sometimes several calls to an individual are needed to get a desired result. However, it's worth it. An automotive company took about fifty inquiries over the course of a year before I finally made it a client, and now it's one of my biggest. Committed to a successful outcome, I put on my calendar to follow up with my contact every week or when I found information or news that could relate to her position at the company. A customer relationship management tool to assist you in following up regularly with people who can help you simplifies the task.

3. *A misunderstanding of business etiquette prevents many entrepreneurs from following up.* The entrepreneur who commits this error is self-absorbed, following up but doing a lousy job at it. An entrepreneur might assume that the contact should always take the next step. Meanwhile, budget planning periods pass, investment priorities change, contacts leave the company, and so on. On the contrary, the entrepreneur who calls back several times, ignoring the "volley protocol," more often gets the prize. Sometimes people simply forget or want you to do all the work, but that's sometimes a small price to pay for a big payoff.

In brief, don't let these three common reasons for failing to follow up cripple you. Entrepreneurs don't miss opportunities; they seize them. The surest way to do this is to follow up with everybody, especially people who can help your business excel. As for the elusive entrepreneur who sought funding from angel investors, his company has not made much progress. No surprise there.

23) Have Laserlike Focus

You must remain focused on your journey to greatness.
—Les Brown, motivational speaker, author

Just a few weeks after being hired, Adam, my vice president of marketing and sales, popped his head into my office through a cracked door and said, "I think we have a problem." After I invited him in, he continued with an easygoing tone that belied the seriousness of his warning, saying, "I think we sell too many things. I find that sales are suffering because we confuse prospects with so many options, and therefore people are less likely to buy." I didn't respond for a few seconds, as I let the veracity of his observations sink in. He was right. My company needed to change; we needed to focus on what we did best instead of trying to be all things to all people.

That day, my company was on the verge of celebrating its ten-year anniversary. The company had come a long way since its founding on a small college campus. In the beginning days of the company, the focus was on building top-notch web applications and offering great value. However, ten years later we had grown to include numerous products and services under the umbrella of a holding company. Consequently, we developed a we-do-it-all mentality and pitch. Our marketing materials, which included pages of options and beautiful examples of our work, were expansive. When it came to media and marketing, if you needed it, we sold it.

Somehow over the ten years of existence, my company lost focus and with it the potential for true greatness. We subscribed to the common idea that expanding our line of products and services was a sure path to more success. It wasn't. As a result, the company wallowed in mediocrity, trying to chase every market possible. Specifically, the quality of our products and services declined, employee morale suffered, resources were wasted, sales leveled off, and confusion abounded. We commoditized ourselves, and we were happy because that's what we thought we were supposed to do.

This idea not only debilitates small and medium-sized businesses, but also large multinational companies. For example, during the 1990s, Apple suffered from an expansive product line that almost led it to bankruptcy. You probably know the story. It took the return of Apple's cofounder, Steve Jobs, as CEO to turn the company around. How did he do it? Jobs eliminated nonessential product lines of the company, keeping only four. Some of his eliminations were profitable lines. Due in large part to its limited focus, Apple is now the most valuable company in the world. When discussing the amazing turnaround in a 2008 interview, Jobs said,

> People think focus means saying "yes" to the thing you've got
> to focus on. But that's not what it means at all. It means saying
> "no" to the hundred other good ideas that there are. You have to
> pick carefully. I'm actually as proud of the things we haven't
> done as the things we have done.

Likewise, Pepsi-Cola stopped trying to be all things to all people in order to compete with its rival Coca-Cola. In their book, *The 21 Immutable Laws of Marketing*, Al Ries and Jack Trout discuss Pepsi-Cola's amazing growth during the 1980s when it changed its focus to reaching the teenage market. Consequently, Pepsi-Cola went from being outsold by Coca-Cola in the late 1950s by five to one to being only 10 percent behind in total sales in the United States. Ries and Trout wrote, "There seems to be an almost religious belief that the wider net catches more customers, in spite of many examples to the contrary."

When my vice president came into my office to tell me that we needed to cut some of our businesses, I quickly reflected on my various entrepreneurial endeavors. At that time I had started fifteen different businesses. All of them had made money at some point, but only a handful were profitable. I realized that I needed to return to my start-up days when my focus was laserlike. That day I learned to say no, as Jobs would have recommended. I cut unnecessary businesses. Since then, my company has enjoyed an invigorating rebirth and growth period that can only be attributed to our willingness to say yes to saying no.

24) Nonprofit Really Means Profit

Opportunity often comes disguised.
—Napoleon Hill, author, *Think and Grow Rich*

When I started my company, I had this ill-conceived notion about nonprofit organizations: I falsely believed that nonprofits weren't worth pursuing as clients. I assumed that they would be terrible customers. After all, they didn't make any profit, right? How could they afford what I had to offer? I was so naïve and dead wrong. Nonprofit organizations were a huge contributor to my early success and continue to be a significant part of my company's revenue.

I learned that for-profit companies and nonprofit organizations have more similarities than differences. For example, nonprofits have the same major challenge that corporations have: generating revenue. In fact, many CEOs and directors of nonprofit organizations lead with a profit mind-set. Furthermore, like corporations, nonprofits devote a large portion of their budgets to purchasing products and services to help generate revenue. This fact translates into opportunity for entrepreneurs to meet that demand. Consequently, nonprofits are likely a viable market for your business.

There are differences, too, between the two entities. Most people focus on the fact that nonprofits use surplus revenues to achieve its goals rather than to distribute them as profit or dividends. In other words, nonprofits *can* have more revenues than expenses in a given fiscal year, but they must use what would be considered profit to fund more programs or to establish an endowment, and so on. Some people classify this difference as a small one, considering that you could interpret a nonprofit organization as a corporation that is reinvesting its surplus back into the business. Nevertheless, the takeaway is that nonprofits certainly have money to spend, just like corporations.

Here are three reasons you should be doing business with nonprofits and perhaps even making them a priority.

1. *Nonprofits do spend money.* A large part of nonprofits' budgets are dedicated to operations, which can include things like utilities, rent, software, training, and travel. They also spend a lot on sales and marketing to find donors or to support ancillary sources of income. According to the *Forbes* list of the 200 largest U.S. charities in 2011, the rankings and annual expenses of five popular charities are as follows:

1. The Mayo Clinic, $5.1 billion
2. YMCAs in the United States, $4.5 billion
3. United Way, $3.8 billion
15. Boys and Girls Clubs, $1.1 billion
20. Habitat for Humanity International, $781 million.

By the way, many nonprofits are required to spend money they received through grants that have very specific guidelines. Certain grants require nonprofits to spend money before a deadline. Thus, an organization may be looking to spend money quickly to remain in compliance with the stipulations of a grant received from a private donor or a government entity.

One of my first major clients was a nonprofit organization in education. My company was able to negotiate an amazing deal in which we received a database of the organization's corporate contacts. It was a list of over one hundred Fortune 500 companies and buyer contact information. In addition to this, the nonprofit organization hired us annually to develop new marketing materials. We also wrote and implemented its social media strategy. This major account lasted nearly a decade, and though we no longer have this client, we still use and benefit from the database of Fortune 500 companies we received.

2. *Nonprofits are willing to take risks with new vendors to save money or to generate solid revenues.* If your product helps nonprofits save money or generate significant income, you are well on your way to gaining great customers. Nonprofits are under constant pressure to watch their spending and keep expenses in check. A quality product or service that aids them in this area is like pure gold.

Shortly after the completion of OmniPublisher, my company's online content management system, we decided to use local nonprofit organizations as our beta testers. We eventually brought many of them on as paying clients and in the process received great feedback on how we could improve our product. Consequently, our first marketing campaign for the software targeted state and national trade organizations that served thousands of nonprofits. The strategy worked well, as many nonprofits loved the product, but more importantly loved the price.

3. *Nonprofits are loyal and will refer you if you are excellent.* In many large cities, you'll find that nonprofits tend to be located in a certain part of the city. Maybe a designated building offers subsidized rent, or that's just where the nonprofit community has thrived. It is a great indication of how close-knit the industry is. Accordingly, executives and employees of different organizations often share resources. They are especially willing to recommend good resources to for-profit enterprises, too.

Over the years, my nonprofit clients have been especially loyal.

They will refer me to other nonprofits and give the most favorable references. I think a common sentiment exists among these organizations that the relationships they build with vendors are special. It's not business as usual in a corporate way. Their vendors help them to save lives, build homes, provide education, and so on. Nonprofit organizations often feel a special affinity for those vendors that help them change the world, and they tend to be especially supportive of their vendors. I have personally witnessed the benefits of this exceeding goodwill, which has helped my company prosper.

If you think that serving the nonprofit sector is a waste of time, just ask Facebook. The social media giant has profited greatly from its popular Causes application. Causes serves hundreds of thousands of nonprofit organizations every day, making Facebook millions of dollars in processing fees and from customizing fundraising campaigns. Not only Facebook, but also many other companies consider the nonprofit sector to be an important business segment. Hence, from the very beginning, see how your product or service can serve nonprofits. Chances are that you will realize that nonprofit really means profit—at least for you.

25) Explore New Adventures for Inspiration

> Exploration is really the essence of the human spirit.
> —Frank Borman, retired NASA astronaut

The other day while checking out new books at Barnes and Noble, I came across the story of how a young Howard Schultz, the current CEO of Starbucks, was inspired by a trip he took to Italy that would change his life completely and change the restaurant business.

In 1981 Schultz was a twenty-eight-year-old director of marketing for Starbucks and in Milan, Italy, on a buying trip. He noticed that not only did the ubiquitous coffee shops there make great espresso, but they also served as local meeting places. These shops were the hubs of the community. Schultz's Italian excursion and the rich experiences he had at those small coffee shops would serve as the model for his aggressive overhaul and growth strategy. We all know the amazing end to this story. Starbucks is now the largest coffeehouse company in the world, with over 19,500 stores in over fifty countries.

This story is just one that proves the benefits of getting outside of your comfort zone, but for many people this is easier said than done. Too often, entrepreneurs operate solely within the confines of their industries. They socialize with the same type of people, go to the same kinds of places, eat the same foods, visit the same websites, read the same books, and speak the same lingo. Or it could be that entrepreneurs are focused on their businesses so much that they don't take time to do something totally unrelated to what they usually do. Immerse yourself in your industry and focus on it, but step away once in a while, too. If you don't, you could be missing out on a monumental, inspirational moment that takes your business to global heights.

Whenever you have the chance to travel, do so. International travel is great, but inspiration can also come from a day trip to another city in your own state or country. Seeing how people do things in a different environment sparks creativity. For example, when visiting Peachtree City here in Georgia, I was amazed to find that the city is designed for residents to drive golf carts everywhere. There is not much need for a car. Small bridges going over main streets and customized paths were built for golf carts. I even saw a mother with her baby hitched to the golf cart in the backseat. I am not sure what business could come from that but I was at least inspired to move there. I thought it was pretty cool.

Stepping outside of your immediate box, whether it's your office or home, also helps to foster inspiration. If I am stumped or experience some sort of a mental block, I step outside my office to take a walk or do an activity that engages another part of my brain or body. A college professor suggested this technique years ago when I was a computer science major. I didn't believe that it worked until I tried it. Whenever I reached a mental block while programming, I would take a break and change my surroundings. Almost magically, a solution to my problem would come to me. As a result, I now use this basic technique frequently to overcome any type of creative breakdown or obstacle.

While the focus has been on changing your scenery for inspiration, exploring new activities is just as important and effective. I have expanded my leisure activities to things I normally would not do, such as learning to speak Chinese, reading classic English literature, and listening to different types of music, like country and Hindi. Ideas for my business now come from the most extraneous experiences. Without making a conscious effort to seek such new things, I doubt these inspirations would have come.

It's hard to believe that a chance trip to Italy brought us Starbucks as we know it today. There isn't a major city on planet Earth that doesn't have a Starbucks. Had Schultz not made that famous trip, who knows where millions of people would buy their coffee in the morning and meet to form a start-up? The evidence is in the coffee, so to speak.

Placing yourself in new environments and exploring new things enables you to apply those experiences to other facets of life. You become a synthesizer, a skill that, honed properly, could be the key to your next big opportunity in business.

26) Failure Doesn't Kill You; It Makes You Stronger

Failure is simply the opportunity to begin again, this time more intelligently.
—Henry Ford, founder, Ford Motor Company

I had the recent privilege of participating in a national business-pitch contest. I entered on a whim, thinking that it would be fun and challenging to put myself in a high-pressure sales situation and see if I could take the top spot. The prize, which was $10,000, would not be so bad either. To my surprise, I was chosen from over one hundred entries across the country to compete against nine other semifinalists in Chicago.

While almost all finalists gave their sixty-second pitch without a hiccup, one finalist completely fell apart under the pressure. It was an utter disaster. Every time he tried to restart his pitch as the big clock counted down the seconds, he would fumble yet again. With each successive attempt, his ability to recover was increasingly difficult. Despite an encouraging and applauding audience of almost one thousand, he eventually gave up. He put his head down and headed off stage to ponder his embarrassing performance. He exited with almost fifteen seconds left on the clock, so the host gently escorted him back to the stage, front and center. The young man's saving grace was the uplifting advice that the three judges gave him after his time expired. He was able to leave the stage with a modicum of self-respect, but you could tell that he was still in shock.

While we were all backstage after the catastrophe, the other finalists and people standing around didn't approach him to offer their support. Instead, they watched him walk by with his head down. He was on the verge of an emotional meltdown as he retreated to a private area backstage to think about what just happened. A few people tried to cheer him up, but their attempts seemed insincere at best. Ironically, the finalists teemed with entrepreneurial confidence but lacked the confidence to show true empathy to a fallen comrade at a crucial moment.

Considering that the dejected finalist was left alone licking his wounds, I approached him to give him a much-needed pep talk. He was about eight years younger than I was, and I sensed that he wasn't very experienced with these types of events. I told him, "You will nail it next time. This is hard to swallow, but you'll recover." I also told him that of all the ideas that I heard in the contest, his was quite promising. I continued, saying, "I would much rather have a terrible pitch from which I can recover than a terrible idea that has no promise." He seemed to agree, but I could tell that he was still depressed for ruining what he considered to be a big opportunity. I could only hope to have made an impact on the young man such that he would pick himself up and keep going. After all, that's what entrepreneurship is all about.

Failure is inevitable in entrepreneurship, but how you deal with failure determines whether you are ultimately a winner. In watching the huge failure of our colleague in this pitch contest, we all were reminded of this reality—a lesson greater than any advice the three judges gave, a lesson more important than the perfect pitch of the winning finalist. Finally, it was a lesson more valuable than winning the $10,000 prize.

27) Seek Partnerships for the Right Reasons

For entrepreneurs looking to build a new business or expand an existing one, a strong partner can be key.
—Barry Horwitz, president, Horwitz & Co.

We had hit a grand slam with one particular partnership. We could hardly contain our excitement. After six months of determining each company's deliverables and getting legal departments to sign off on the agreement, our partnership with a global company with billions of dollars in assets was on the verge of becoming reality.

We could now accelerate our growth, using our partner's many global channels. We felt as if we hit the jackpot and were just waiting to receive our bags of money. Then things suddenly grew complicated.

After the company's sales director signed off on the deal and encouraged us to post a press release on our website with a quotation that he provided, I received the following message in an e-mail: "This email is to confirm there is no national partnership agreement with our company and . . . the press release you have currently posted on your national web site is wrong and misleading. Please remove it from your web site today." I also received a threatening phone call from the senior vice president of the company, asking me to call her immediately. When I called, she demanded that we remove our press release and disregard any agreements made by her colleagues; otherwise we would face their legal department.

I knew we had a major problem, but whatever the problem was, it wasn't with my company. We had made sure to get permission in writing for everything we wanted to do. My best guess was that something had happened internally at the other company to cause the partnership to fall apart. Despite the collapse of the deal, a part of me was happy that it occurred before we were too involved. After the incident, we had no desire to work with the company. So, the result was no world denomination for us or trips to the bank for our money bags—at least not with this shoddy partner.

I later found out that the pernicious partner wasn't really able to open doors that we thought it could. The company had several affiliates that had tremendous power over headquarters. In other words, because individual owners had the final say of working with my company, there was no value in partnering with the parent company. Even with the endorsement of the potential partner's headquarters, we would still have to convince affiliate owners of the value of working with us. Moreover, the partner's endorsement would strain its relationships with unwilling owners. We didn't anticipate this scenario, especially since the true relationship between the parent company and affiliates wasn't clear. Regardless, our intentions and proceedings were transparent. If the partner had operated the same way, everything would have gone smoothly.

If put together properly, partnerships can significantly boost your business. The key to establishing an effective partnership is best described by start-up guru Guy Kawasaki: "The gist of good partnering is that it should accelerate cash flow, increase revenue, and reduce costs. Partnerships built on solid business principles like these have a much greater likelihood of succeeding."

However, a partnership built improperly wastes your time and hurts your business. As Kawasaki suggests, some reasons not to form a partnership include covering your weaknesses and generating press coverage. These are two sure ways to start off on the wrong foot, but several entrepreneurs believe that these are perfectly tenable reasons to pursue a partnership. Partnerships should be built on strengths, not weaknesses. Each company's goal should be to enhance something the other company does well. Furthermore, partnerships established to impress or placate the press inevitably backfire. Sooner or later, the true intentions of the partnership surface, especially if it's yielded no tangible results.

In short, partnerships should not be taken lightly or rushed, and they should be pursued for the right reasons. If you follow the suggested guidelines, you will be less likely to enter into a partnership that does more harm than good. As for the botched partnership I mentioned earlier, we found another partner with a global presence. This relationship has worked out great, and revenues have increased over 700 percent.

28) Be a Master at Leveraging Resources

---

*People with leverage have dominance over people with
less leverage.*
—Robert T. Kiyosaki, author, *Rich Dad, Poor Dad*

When I started my media company, very few prospects wanted to
buy advertisements. They saw the tremendous value in my media
outlets, but always tried to leverage what they had instead of paying. For example, I approached a Chinese restaurant near my college campus that offered me a semester's worth of free food in exchange for advertisement. A few blocks down from the restaurant,
there was a shoe store. The owner there promised to give me six
pairs of new shoes for each ad I ran for him. I could go on for a
long time, listing the things that I was offered instead of hard cash.
The perks were great—I was never hungry or barefoot—but they
didn't help me pay for operations. It would have been hard to pay
for printing, web hosting, and distribution with a sweet and sour
combo and a pair of Fila.

Frustrated and perplexed I asked my mentor how to actually get
money for my products and services. Frankly I never considered
the possibility of such a problem. I assumed that everyone would
pay me money. The whole idea of bartering or trading was new to
me. It seemed unprofessional and somewhat shady. A part of me
thought that people were taking advantage of me, hoping that I
would take whatever they offered. My mentor had a different perspective.

When I approached my mentor for advice, the most recent request for a trade deal was from a major movie studio. It wanted to
place an ad for an upcoming movie in exchange for giving me several movie passes to the premier. This seemed like a terrible deal to
me. I complained to my mentor that I had limited advertising space
and that I wanted to reserve insertions for paying customers only.
My mentor smiled and said, "Kevin, run a small ad for them and

take the passes." He explained how I could use the passes in various ways. I thought one was especially clever. He suggested that I give some of the passes to a major radio station in the city. In exchange, the radio station would give away the passes to listeners on the air on my behalf. I would also ask the station to encourage listeners to consider advertising with my company. That way, I could increase my media's brand presence, establish strong relationships with the station, and reach thousands of potential advertisers. When he explained all of this, I got really excited. I took his advice, and everything worked out just as he said it would.

After receiving and taking his advice, my perspective changed completely. Suddenly, selling became more fun because I didn't see myself as a salesman, per se, but as a person who creatively leveraged resources to get more of what I wanted. I learned that many of the smaller or local companies wanted to keep their cash, especially since I was a new vendor. It helped them to offset risk. Larger companies didn't mind paying the cash. After realizing that, I began to use my local perks to entice the big companies for more advertisements. For instance, instead of taking all six pairs of shoes from my shoe advertiser, I would only take two. The other four pair I would use to secure long-term advertising contracts with Fortune 100 companies. In other words, the people responsible for signing the contracts would receive some nice sneakers for their children as a thank-you.

I have structured so many deals in which I strategically used products and services that companies have offered me instead of money. I have used professional sporting event tickets, tee times, lavish trips, concert tickets, and other things to find my way to a bigger check that justifies my approach. It is probably the most fun and creative part of what I do. Out of this practice, I developed a love of putting together deals, whether it's a basic trade or a buyout worth millions of dollars.

This strategy works the other way, too. If you want to conserve your cash, find ways to leverage what you have to get what you want. For example, I was able to secure a deal with a multimillion-aire simply by offering to make a substantial donation to his charity. That check, while significant, was much less than the check I would have had to write in order to secure his involvement in the deal the normal way. This type of creativity pays both ways.

As you begin to implement this strategy, be very careful not to overdo it. Choose only certain companies to engage in this type of arrangement. You must be strategic about every deal and understand the motives and desires of all parties involved. A common problem is that once a vendor knows that you are willing to trade or do nontraditional deals, you may be held to that standard or less. Thus, you run the risk of being able to change expectations about types of payment and terms. Also, influencers in the same circles may share the details of your deal with others who under normal circumstances would pay you.

Finally, entrepreneurs are great at leveraging resources to get what they want. When one competitor shuns the idea of a trade or nontraditional deal, another competitor accepts it and uses it as an advantage. This strategy has worked wonders for me over the years. In fact, I still have pairs of brand-new shoes in my closet that were given to me as part of a deal almost seven years ago. I won't need a new pair for probably another seven years.

29) An Idea's Execution, Not Its Uniqueness, Yields Success

Ideas are easy. It's the execution of ideas that really separates the sheep from the goats.
—Sue Grafton, author

I hate to rain on your parade, but your idea is not special. There are likely other entrepreneurs or companies with "your" idea, equally inspired to dominate the business world and to make millions.

And when your idea becomes a solid business generating lots of revenue, you can be sure that someone is just waiting to capitalize on your idea, too. In Silicon Valley, copycat companies are called "me-too" companies. You know them. For instance, once Groupon became popular, all sorts of me-too companies sprang up. According to a recent MSNBC.com report, over six hundred companies have the same business model as Groupon or a variation on it.

Despite the fact that your idea is not unique and thus for the taking, you can still boost your probability of success over your competitors. How? Focus on the execution of your idea and make it work better than anyone else on the planet.

When I was in college, everyone had my idea: Create a web-based community for the consortium of colleges and universities in Atlanta. Even after my website became hugely popular, some students would belittle my accomplishments when they met me. They would say things like, "I had that idea." Or they would comment matter-of-factly, "I wanted to do that." I didn't take their snubs to heart, because I knew that the implication of their comments was true: My idea wasn't special. In fact, I considered their comments to be a sincere compliment, because I knew that I actually had the determination to make the idea a reality. They didn't.

A gap the size of the Grand Canyon separates idea and execution. Most people, when they see the huge abyss before them and ponder the work needed to traverse it, never make a move. They are paralyzed for a myriad of reasons. It could be the enormity of the task, the lack of skills needed to get to the other side, or fear of the unknown. Whatever the reason, those who execute their idea and get to the other side of the canyon will be winners.

In order to go from idea to execution and thus secure a major advantage over your competition, pay close attention to three things that were largely responsible for my early success: speed, team, and frugality.

First, *the speed of your organization, especially in our fast-paced, technology-driven, I-want-it-now world, is most important.* You must focus on shortening your time to market. When you do this, you stake your claim in the marketplace first and are able to sell to customers before others. It's a delicate balance, though, between speed and quality. Your goal should be to release immediately a functional and a somewhat quality product or service that customers value. Founder of LinkedIn, Reid Hoffman, said, "If you are not embarrassed by the first version of your product, you've launched too late." Well said. In college, my team and I were never fully satisfied with the software we produced, but we understood the need to get the customer using it quickly. We'd have plenty of time later for upgrades and improvements.

Second, *your team must be a well-oiled machine that works harder than any other team.* The advice is trite but cannot be emphasized enough. Team dynamics can make or break you. Only recruit the best and most dedicated talent that is vested in your idea. Likewise, avoid debilitating deputes over equity and the company's direction. In his book *The Founder's Dilemma*, Harvard professor Noam Wasserman explores common problems that founders go through when starting their companies. Wasserman provides scholarly research on team dynamics and equity splits among team members. As his extensive research proved, if you don't get your team right, the probability of your success drops drastically.

Third, *a frugal start-up is a wise start-up.* Expenses frequently hinder a company's ability to execute an idea. The company that can conserve and best use its resources gives itself a considerable advantage. As young entrepreneurs, my team and I decided to take a grassroots approach to everything we did. For example, we used free, open-source technologies to develop our products. Likewise, we leveraged our campus contacts to print thousands of signs that advertised our website. The expenses we incurred to make our idea a reality were as close to zero as a company could get. Even when we had money coming in, we continued to operate with a frugal mentality. As a result, when we absolutely needed to spend money to generate growth, we had it and could move fast.

A common perception of an entrepreneur is the idea-generating, dream-chasing idealist. This one-sided view overlooks the equally important part of the entrepreneur that is an unyielding execution-er. Facebook's cofounder Mark Zuckerberg had a big vision to "dominate" communication on the Internet, and he could communicate his perspective better than anyone. He also knew how to make that vision happen—and he made it happen. If you are banking on the merit of your idea and not the efficiency of its execution, you are headed for trouble. You will probably end up like the people who begrudged my success in college, saying, "I had that idea."

30) Find an Enemy

A man can't be too careful in the choice of his enemies.
—Oscar Wilde, Irish writer, poet

One of the biggest rivalries in business history is between Apple and Microsoft, two behemoths that have ruled the technology sector for decades. Wherever you go in the world, whether it's to the United States or to China, you find the same scenario: Apple users hate Microsoft users and vice versa.

Even the founders of these two companies shared a personal rivalry tantamount to an East Coast–West Coast rapper feud. On the one hand, cofounder of Apple Steve Jobs said this about the co-founder of Microsoft Bill Gates: "Bill is basically unimaginative and has never invented anything, which is why I think he's more comfortable now in philanthropy than technology. He just shame-lessly ripped off other people's ideas." On the other hand, Gates had this to say about Jobs: "[Steve Jobs] really never knew much about technology, but he had an amazing instinct for what works." Gates also called Jobs "fundamentally odd" and "weirdly flawed." The evidence of these two founders' mutual disdain is quite obvi-ous. (And if you were wondering, I suppose Jobs would be Tupac Shakur and Gates would be The Notorious B.I.G.)

Like Apple and Microsoft, there are numerous other rivalries in business. Just to name a few, there's Coca-Cola and Pepsi-Cola, McDonald's and Burger King, Ford and General Motors, Verizon and AT&T, the Boston Red Sox and the New York Yankees, and the list continues. All of these companies fight one another for market share and world domination. It can get pretty dirty, too, with firms spying on and suing one another. Despite the negatives, these fierce rivalries have a benefit that is seldom mentioned: They fuel a competitive environment that motivates each company to excel. Entrepreneurs should be well aware of this phenomenon and how to use it to their advantage.

As publisher of an Atlanta magazine, I made sure to find and identify an enemy quickly, and the strategy worked well. Although we had many enemies, we singled out one publication that we ut-terly hated. Our goal was to put it out of business. Although we didn't put it out of business, we did make the competitive land-scape more intense. We made sure that everything we produced was exponentially better in quality than our enemy's work. In fact, my magazine's success eventually caused our main competitor to increase its costs by printing in color. We knew that we were win-ning at that point. As a result of this noticeable change, my team became even more excited and motivated to trample the competition.

When you start a business, immediately choose an enemy that you and your team aspire to crush. Identifying an archrival helps to solidify your team around a common goal and serves as a natural motivator. No one wants to lose in a game of one-on-one. It's one thing to rally a team around stodgy goals like increasing sales 35 percent for the quarter; it's another to rally a team around a tangible enemy that hates you as much as you hate them. Implementing this basic gamification strategy enhances your competitive spirit and at least makes business a lot more exciting for everybody.

31) Don't Underestimate Your Competition

I hate competition.
—Marat Safin, tennis champion, Russian politician

When entrepreneurs approach me to invest in their companies, I naturally want to know who their competitors are. It's a basic question that any investor would ask.

Some entrepreneurs answer the question thoroughly and confidently. They are not afraid to acknowledge what the competitive landscape looks like. Others equivocate, either because they don't want the fact that competitors exist to diminish the appeal of their idea or they simply haven't done their homework.

Of the two responses, I am more concerned about and hesitant toward entrepreneurs who seem delusional or unprepared. They often respond to my inquiry, proudly saying, "We do not have any competitors."

I want to respond to them, "Yeah, right."

The answer that they gave to make their venture appear more attractive actually made it more unattractive. Instead of telling them what I'd like to say, I keep quiet and focus on companies that are better suited for investment.

Theoretically, every company in a free market has competition, even if it is pioneering a completely new market category. A customer's dollar can be spent in millions of ways, and with millions of businesses. The competition may not be obvious or simple to find, but it's there. Your job as an entrepreneur is to find and to assess the most threatening competition. A more in-depth step includes identifying and analyzing companies that could easily leverage their resources—like distribution channels, investment capital, or intellectual capital—to enter your market and to compete with you.

A common mistake that mostly start-ups make when researching their competition is overlooking substitutes. What are substitutes? According to N. Gregory Mankiw, an economist from Harvard University, "Substitutes are often pairs of goods that are used in place of each other, such as hot dogs and hamburgers, sweaters and sweatshirts, and movie tickets and video rentals." Substitutes can also be defined as "two goods for which an increase in the price of one leads to an increase in the demand for the other." Substitutes can harm a company, especially in a price war.

Often entrepreneurs focus only on other companies that have very similar business models. To expand on the examples given in the definition, a hot dog company may only research other hot dog companies, a sweater company may only research other sweater companies, and so on. This myopic perspective ignores the competitive threat of dissimilar substitutes and can cause the downfall of a good company.

For example, it could be argued that Blockbuster's demise occurred because it failed to adequately assess the threat of a substitute, Netflix, which was the first company to offer a DVD-by-mail service. As the price of Blockbuster's video rental services increased, so did the demand of Netflix's services, which were so much more convenient than walking into a brick-and-mortar store. Had Blockbuster correctly assessed the threat in the beginning, it would have had a better chance to survive by implementing its own DVD-by-mail service. Instead, it increased its video rental prices and didn't introduce a DVD-by-mail service until 2004, years after Netflix had seized a large portion of the market.

Never tell a potential investor that you have absolutely no competition. Any seasoned investor interprets such a statement as, "These guys are full of themselves and naïve enough to think that they have no competition. This is a waste of my time." Instead, introduce your competition, but describe the severity of the competitive threat. Moreover, no matter if you are in the initial stages of developing your start-up or if you are a developed company, don't underestimate the competitive threat of substitutes. Committing either one of these mistakes will likely cause you to have a Blockbuster ending.

32) Ask for What You Want

Ask and it will be given to you.
—Matthew 7:7

While driving on the major freeway that runs through the heart of Atlanta, I saw a huge banner on the side of a mid-rise. The banner promoted the grand opening of a new residential building in Midtown, a popular and prime area of the city. Considering that the building had vacancies, I thought that the owner would be a great prospective advertiser for one of my media outlets that target young adults. I wrote down the phone number and website listed on the banner and reached out a few days later. Within no time, I was able to set up a meeting with the builder and leasing agent.

After a brief meeting I closed the sale rather quickly. My intuition paid off. At the time, it was one of the biggest deals I had ever closed. I was especially excited about the deal, but I dreamed of having more. I thought, *How cool would it be to have an office here, right in the center of town with a spectacular view of the Atlanta skyline?* For a second I pondered asking the builder if I could have one of the large units as an office. I thought that the idea was ridiculous, but then I remembered some of the stories my mentor told me about how he was able to close some out-of-this-world deals. I changed my mind. Since I had already finalized the deal, I figured that it wouldn't hurt to ask. So I asked the owner of the building, "May I have one of the units to use as an office?" The builder replied, "Sure. That's not a problem at all." In addition to paying me well for my company's services, he gave me one of the best units in his building.

Within a few weeks I was moving into my brand-new, thirteen-hundred-square-foot, fully furnished office for my company. It was quite a space, with a perfect location and beautiful views of the city. In fact, the office was located across the street from PricewaterhouseCoopers and Google's new office. This new space would serve as my company's headquarters for a few years. My ten-person team and I loved it. If I had stayed quiet and let my doubts take over, I would have missed this great opportunity.

When I started my business I had no idea of the possibilities that would be available to me. I never imagined that I would be given a beautiful office space in a prime, urban location simply by asking. Neither did I imagine that I would be able to simply ask a client for a luxury car and receive it. After closing some amazing deals by just asking for what I wanted, my expectations for what was possible changed completely. I learned that when the scope of your reality is limited by your experience, it's hard to imagine anything beyond it. Once I widened the scope of my reality, I was able to negotiate unbelievable deals.

As I alluded to earlier, my mentor taught me to ask for what I want in business. He believed that nothing was impossible. Without his guidance, I would have missed several opportunities simply because I was too afraid to ask for them. For some reason, perhaps because of my young age, I didn't think that I deserved them. Thankfully, my mentor was able to open my mind to bigger ideas and to show me through his own experiences what was possible. Ultimately, I learned that there's a big difference between thinking and knowing what is possible versus having the courage to ask for it. If you want something, I encourage you to ask for it. You will be surprised to see what it gets you from time to time.

33) No Competition Means Your Idea Probably Has Little Merit

Competition is very good. . . . It's what makes one strive to be better.
—Christine Lahti, actress, film director

Ninety-five percent of the time, arrogance leads entrepreneurs to believe that they have no competition in the marketplace. However, on rare occasions, arrogance isn't the true cause of this belief. Instead, arrogance is an effect of a more basic cause, and veterans of business know this. What's the cause? It's actually a thorough and accurate assessment of the current competitive environment that yields no competitors. The difference, though, is that arrogant entrepreneurs think that the nonexistence of competition means sure success while veterans know that this likely means that the idea is not viable for various reasons.

Considering this, entrepreneurs must learn how to interpret the results of their research on competition when it produces no threats. Assuming that no threats were identified and that your research methodology was solid, you must take your market research to the next level, which includes discovering specific reasons that an idea has no competitors. The most common and important reason is that the idea isn't good. The four most common reasons that a business idea is unfeasible and therefore has no competitors in the market are as follows:

1. *No demand exists for the product.* For example, due to low demand, the DeLorean, a futuristic sports car that debuted in 1981, was a failure. In fact, few people today know that the DeLorean was indeed a real car and not just a fictitious, flying car in the pop-

ular *Back to the Future* movie series, which began four years later. Apparently, when the DeLorean hit the market, there was little demand for an overpriced sports car that went from 0 to 60 mph in a slow 10.5 seconds. The magazine *Road and Track* gave the car a poor review, saying, "It's not a barn burner." Perhaps the *Back to the Future* series was on to something—if only the makers of the DeLorean could go back in time and warn themselves that their invention would be a flop because of lack of demand.

2. *The market is too small.* Perhaps the most recent surprising example of a market being too small is the story of the Segway, the two-wheeled electric vehicle that was all the excitement before its launch in 2001. What was once the most anticipated invention to the hit the market is now all but a complete failure. The company that produces the vehicle expected sales to reach as much as one hundred thousand units within the first thirteen months, but it didn't even come close. In a stark contrast to company expectations, only about thirty thousand Segways were sold between 2001 and 2007. Segway greatly overestimated the market size for its new category of vehicle, and thus its signature product has become a novelty, not the revolutionary means of transportation it was proclaimed to be.

3. *The business is not profitable.* How long is too long to wait for profits? Two years? Five? Ten? Well, for the hipster car-rental company Zipcar, the wait for profits will have to be longer than twelve years. The company has yet to make a profit since its founding in 2000, and it doesn't look like profits will arrive any time soon. According to *The New York Times*, Zipcar has accumulated losses of $65.4 million, including a net loss of $14.7 million in 2010. How long one should wait to reap profits is debatable, but what isn't debatable is the fact that profits are an important measure of success. After all, you are in business to make a profit. At some point you run out of possible adjustments or lose hope that the market will develop. A business that isn't profitable, let alone not profitable for twelve years, is a red flag.

4. *The barriers to entry are too great*. The pharmaceutical industry in the United States has quite a few high hurdles that make it difficult to enter into the enormous drug market. Perhaps one of the biggest and most unpredictable hurdles is the Food and Drug Administration, a government agency that approves and regulates new drugs. In 2011, Contrave, a weight-loss drug developed by Orexigen Therapeutics, was denied FDA approval—a huge blow to the company. According to *The New York Times*, the FDA told the drugmaker that to win approval it must first do a long-term study to demonstrate that the drug does not raise the risk of heart attacks. Hundreds of millions of dollars are at stake as the company regroups. Investors hope to get the drug approved as soon as possible to recoup their investments. To that the FDA would reply, "Fat chance!"

In short, no competition probably means you have a bad business idea on your hands. There are several reasons for bad business ideas, but these four are quite common and useful to remember, especially when analyzing a barren marketplace. Therefore, each one warrants your special attention. Often what looks like a harmless path to success is really a dangerous path leading you right off a cliff.

34) Put Out Fires Quickly

The man who has no problems is out of the game.
—Elbert Hubbard, writer, philosopher

When checking my e-mail one morning, I noticed an urgent subject: "Web Site Down. Call Immediately." This wasn't a good sign. I knew then that it was going to be a long day—and it was.

Until that moment, I had never had a customer contact me about a major problem with a product my company created. I didn't know what to do. No one had told me how to deal with an irate customer. I was learning on the job.

The disgruntled customer was a major media company. Only a year after I started my company, this customer took a chance and bought the first version of our content management system, OmniPublisher. The company used the software to produce the online version of its newspaper. OmniPublisher included web hosting through a third-party vendor, and that was the problem.

Just a few months after the media company purchased our web-based software, I received the fateful e-mail notifying me that the company's administrative website was down. Apparently, our web hosting partner was having a problem with its servers, preventing our customers from making updates to their site. Even worse, our clients' readership couldn't access the clients' sites. All visitors saw the dreaded and embarrassing Error 404 page.

I immediately contacted our client's chief technology officer and told him that we were taking care of the situation. I didn't want to make that call, because I expected a tongue-lashing. It wasn't so bad after all. He appreciated my swift response to his e-mail but was eager to get the problem resolved. I spent all day putting pressure on the web host to fix their servers. I couldn't do much else, except wait for the vendor and mitigate the situation with the customer by offering concessions. I was stressed like never before. The web host eventually fixed the servers that evening. As a result, my company made changes to its web host plan and learned a valuable lesson about responding to customer complaints.

Most importantly, we formalized the way we handle urgent, customer complaints. We use this simple five-step process:

1. Respond quickly and calmly.
2. Listen attentively after you offer a sincere apology.
3. Tell the customer how you plan to address the problem in detail with a specific time frame.
4. Give updates often on the progress of your resolution.
5. When the issue is resolved, make sure the customer is satisfied.

Not only will this process help you to handle similar problems in a professional way, but it will also provide a guideline by which you can evaluate the effectiveness of your response.

To be great in business means to be great at putting out fires quickly. They are inevitable, and one of the biggest fires you'll have to put out is an urgent customer complaint. Making sure that you resolve customer complaints in the best way possible, so as to ensure that customers stay with your company, should not be something you learn while on the job, if you can help it. Prepare for the fire, and your chances of avoiding a customer conflagration will be much better.

35) Have an Exit Strategy

Begin with the end in mind.
—Stephen Covey, best-selling author, *The Seven Habits of Highly Effective People*

When I shut down my college magazine (my third business), it had lasted six good years. During its run, the magazine was declared one of the top independent college magazines in the country. The last issue was published in 2008 just a few months before the beginning of the Great Recession, which also took down several other publications, big and small. At that point, advertising sales for the publishing industry came to a screeching halt, a harbinger of things to come. If I knew what I know now, I would have sold my magazine in 2007 after its record year of revenues in 2006. As they say, hindsight is 20/20.

I didn't sell the magazine because I made the mistake of believing that I would always be interested in keeping the business. I also assumed that I would want to be in the print publishing business forever. I was wrong. Around the same time that the market tanked, I was ready to get rid of the business, and I didn't enjoy print publishing nearly as much as when I started. As a result of the confluence of the recession and my eagerness to get out of the business, my magazine just died. I made no real attempts to sell it or even give it away. Even if I had made a legitimate effort to sell it, the market conditions would have made it next to impossible to pull it off. Sadly, all was lost.

Having learned the hard way, I now start a business with an exit in mind. Unfortunately, few young entrepreneurs take the same approach. In fact, a recent survey conducted by Pricewaterhouse-Coopers found that only 54 percent of business owners within five years of retirement had an exit strategy. For businesses with revenues under $10 million, only 30 percent had an exit strategy.

Considering these alarming statistics, you probably have not considered an exit strategy for your business. In other words, you could end up like me, having to watch your business die at some point without getting the value out of it. Or you could sell your business for less than its true value. Both situations can be avoided if you plan ahead.

The biggest benefit to planning your exit from the very beginning is that it helps you to make good decisions for your business. For example, had I planned an exit, I would have been looking for opportune times to sell my magazine. I would have realized, after reaching record profits in 2006 and after the tremendous growth in popularity of digital devices and digital advertising, that it was the perfect time to cash out. Of course, there is no guarantee that I would have avoided the Great Recession, but at least I would have given myself a chance to pursue great opportunities.

As one of my favorite entrepreneurs, Earvin "Magic" Johnson, said, "If you fail to plan your exit strategy, you can pretty much plan on failing." Johnson knows what he is talking about, as he has sold many businesses and continues to build his business empire. In 2010 Johnson sold his 4.5 percent equity stake in the Los Angeles Lakers, making a huge profit. He knew it was time to move on to bigger things, like purchasing the Los Angeles Dodgers recently for $2 billion.

Magic Johnson is one example of several elite entrepreneurs who seem to have impeccable timing and good fortune, but when you look closer, you find the secret to their success: an exit strategy planned from day one. Despite how awkward or how uncomfortable it may be, plan an exit strategy when you start your business. Smart entrepreneurs not only focus on creating their business but also plan how to get out of it the best way possible.

Chapter 2

Education

Formal education will make you a living; self-education
will make you a fortune.
—Jim Rohn, entrepreneur, author, motivational speaker

When you become an entrepreneur, your education is just beginning. In fact, in order to be at the top of your game, you must continually seek and devour information that will make you and your business better. An entrepreneur who stops learning stops earning.

Unfortunately, most secondary schools and colleges don't teach how to attain entrepreneurial success. For this reason, some of the most successful entrepreneurs left school early, eager to gain real-world experience. Entrepreneurs educate themselves primarily through reading books, studying successful people, perusing industry magazines, attending conferences, and countless other ways.

In this brief chapter, you learn how too much formal education can be a hindrance and how your ability to educate yourself affects your bottom line.

---

36) School Is Not Necessarily Education

Develop a passion for learning. If you do, you will never cease to grow.
—Anthony J. D'Angelo, entrepreneur, education trailblazer

When I arrived at Morehouse College, I was focused on doing well in my classes so that I could get a high-paying job as a computer programmer. After catching the entrepreneurial bug during my sophomore year, I was just trying to graduate with a decent GPA. At that point, school was a barrier, a prison preventing me from doing full-time what I loved. I vividly remember sitting in one of my core classes—religion, to be exact—and feeling trapped. That day I tuned out the professor, pulled out a piece of paper, and began working on computer algorithms. I felt that I was learning so much more pursuing my entrepreneurial endeavors. I had had enough of school. When I graduated, I was ready to sprint off campus.

It turns out that my experience is common among entrepreneurs. In his book *The Millionaire Mind*, Dr. Thomas J. Stanley dedicates forty-five pages to describe the school days of America's millionaires. A great majority of them are self-made entrepreneurs. He writes, "Millionaires also report that they were not A students in college. In fact, only about three in ten reported receiving a greater percentage of As than either Bs, Cs, Ds, or Fs. About 90 percent graduated from college. Overall, their GPA was a 2.9— good but not outstanding." Likewise, Dr. Stanley found that most millionaires did well on the SAT, but not excellent. His research confirmed that characteristics other than great school performance were more significant factors in most millionaires' success. Some of these characteristics include being honest, disciplined, amiable, and diligent, and having great leadership skills.

Realizing that there is actually a negative correlation between the amount of schooling after college and entrepreneurial success, some wealthy individuals discourage students from pursuing school if they have entrepreneurial talents and great ideas at an early age. Most recently, Peter Thiel, the billionaire cofounder of PayPal and angel investor, started his innovative and shocking program that pays students to drop out of college. His program chose four bright college students who show amazing entrepreneurial promise and funded each of their companies with $100,000. Thiel said in an interview with ABC News, "Learning is good. Credentialing and debt is very bad. College gives people learning and also takes away future opportunities by loading the next generation down with debt." I can relate to Thiel's quotation. Many of my friends would love to start a business but are stuck with high student loan payments that could be used as start-up capital. I was fortunate to receive a full scholarship from NASA to attend college. Without this boon I probably would not have chosen the entrepreneurial path.

Considering the frustrating experience of my college days, the compelling data from *The Millionaire Mind*, and the popularity of Peter Thiel's college dropout program, you may believe that I support young entrepreneurs dropping out of college or forgetting college altogether. I do not. College is an important experience for entrepreneurs. People often point out that Mark Zuckerberg and other successful entrepreneurs dropped out of college, but their examples *did* at some point attend college. As in Zuckerberg's case, there were huge benefits from attending college. We can all agree that Facebook wouldn't be what it is without Zuckerberg's Harvard experience. David Kilpatrick, author of *The Facebook Effect*, says, "Facebook's ultimate success owes a lot to the fact that it began at college. That's where people's social networks are densest." I couldn't agree more, given that I started my first profitable business for college students in college.

The passionate debate persists about whether college and advanced degrees are worth it for entrepreneurs. However, everyone can agree that although you may not be in school, your education should never stop. Entrepreneurs who excel educate themselves constantly about new technology, business strategies, and so on, and you don't necessarily have to be in school to do that.

37) You're in No Rush to Get an MBA

"You wasted $150,000 on an education you could have got for a buck fifty in late charges at the public library."
—Matt Damon, in *Good Will Hunting*

When I was introduced by my student host, I stood up and briefly addressed the room full of second-year Harvard Business School students from all around the world. Surprisingly, I was the only prospective student among a handful to stand up during the pre-class introduction, adhering to what I thought was proper and respectful protocol. The other visitors were shy and perhaps a bit intimidated by the Ivy League crowd. Because of my display of confidence and cordiality, I received the warmest welcome from the students. In fact, when my host mentioned that I attended Morehouse College, a few students shouted with excitement. Other than this warm reception and conversation with students between classes, my campus visit to Harvard Business School in April 2007 was much different than I had imagined.

That morning, April 12, I arrived at Harvard Business School a few minutes behind schedule. I forgot that the business school is separate from the main Harvard campus; it is located on the opposite side of the Charles River, perhaps a not-so-subtle indication of its lofty status. After calling admissions and receiving directions from a rather unpleasant administrator, I found my meeting place: the Dillon House. From there, a student host took me to class with her. On the way she answered my questions and introduced me to some of her friends. After attending class I found some old college friends who were now HBS students, and they took me to lunch. We passionately debated and discussed the meaning of life and the classic book *The 48 Laws of Power*. Following that I walked around, taking in the sights and smells; visited the Coop or HBS bookstore, buying an HBS T-shirt; managed to get lost in the underground tunnels, trying to avoid the snow; and ended up in the library, reading my *FORTUNE Small Business* magazine while waiting for my ride. That was my visit.

At the time, attending business school to get my MBA was not a top priority. After college I was not eager to go back to school at all. Instead, I wanted to continue as a fearless young entrepreneur, growing my business and pursing opportunities that required my full energy and resources. However, I eventually caved to the pressure of my peers, who thought it was the logical thing to do. Also, my parents encouraged me to get a graduate degree because "the longer I waited, the harder it would be to return." And I had a highly inflated self-image. What better way to massage my ego than to obtain an MBA from Harvard Business School! So I made the trip to Boston, where I grew up, in hopes that a campus visit would increase my excitement for HBS in particular, and for graduate school in general.

Shockingly, the campus visit did more harm than good. The ivy-clad campus, known for its charm and majesty, had a gloomy effect on me. I found it to be off-putting and uninspiring. Furthermore, the classes I attended were perfunctory and boring. I am afraid to admit it, but I almost fell asleep during one class titled Leadership Accountability and Ethics. In this class, it seemed that no substantive conversation took place, as if the professor and students were just talking to hear themselves talk. I am sure that there were some redeeming characteristics of the school, but I surely missed them. It could have been that I was out of my league. Regardless, I left the campus visit highly disappointed and eager to head home, back to the exciting life of a start-up CEO. At the end of that day I realized that my presence was a sign of my giving up or at best putting on hold my entrepreneurial dreams.

Attending Harvard Business School at that time, if I were accepted, would have been a mistake. I would have been completely miserable and frustrated. In the same way that college almost smothered my fiery ambition to pursue entrepreneurship, graduate school would have strangled me. I would have eventually succumbed to the luring pull of a high-paying consulting job or chosen to crunch numbers for a New York hedge fund. Not even the prestige and countless benefits of receiving a Harvard MBA were going to pull me away from my business and doing what I loved.

Since then, I continue to consider going back to school, but not just to get a degree. Now that I am a little wiser, I have a genuine interest in the knowledge taught; I aspire to learn as much as I can about the business world, and academia is a great place to do that in a focused environment. I recently read Philip Delves Broughton's book *Ahead of the Curve,* which chronicles his life-altering experience as an HBS student. I have also talked to friends who have their degrees from Harvard and other great business schools. Many of them still struggle to find gratifying jobs. In fact, many of them discourage me from going. I agree with them. After weighing all the costs, I am still not convinced of the value. The only way I will seriously consider it is if I receive a full scholarship and if I can continue to run my business.

In the meantime, I do what all successful entrepreneurs do: learn as much as possible about business constantly. That includes subscribing to industry magazines, reading white papers, attending conferences, interviewing experts, examining case studies, and so on. Entrepreneurs fervently seek knowledge to gain and to maintain a competitive advantage for their business.

One of my mentors heard I was considering Harvard Business School and scolded me. He said, "What would that degree do for you? You'd ultimately go back to running your business. You'd lose time and money. You don't need Harvard; Harvard needs you!" Ignoring his head-inflating words, my mentor's argument made pragmatic sense. Considering my unique situation, the opportunity cost of going to school would be too great. In fact, attending school could kill my business altogether. At that point, I realized that obtaining my MBA would probably not be in my near future. Given that, I decided to resort to the next best thing: Hiring business school graduates to help me run my business. So far, it has worked out great.

Chapter 3

People

"I love humanity. It's people I can't stand."
—Linus van Pelt, in *Peanuts*

In his classic book *How to Win Friends and Influence People*, Dale Carnegie mentions Charles Schwab, one of the first in American business to earn an annual salary more than $1 million. Schwab attributed his high salary to his ability to deal with people. As the first president of the newly formed United States Steel Company in 1921, he had amazing charisma and enthusiasm that inspired his employees to greatness.

The story of Charles Schwab's ascendancy in business underlines the importance of dealing with people in any business. As an entrepreneur, your ability to repel bad people and to attract good people, whether in the office or in your bedroom, makes all the difference in your level of success.

In this chapter, you learn what matters most when dealing with people, so that you can surround yourself with the kind of people who move your business forward.

---

38) Spend the Majority of Your Time with People Smarter Than You

As iron sharpens iron, so one man sharpens another.
—Proverbs 27:17

The average person is intimidated by smart people. I know firsthand: Whenever people find out what I scored on an SAT exam, they are shocked. (I have very proud relatives.) Some try to stump me on the spot with a complex riddle or math question. Others just look at me in disbelief or with gut-wrenching jealousy. I can sense their fear of being judged. They watch their grammar and double-check their math; some point out a major accomplishment of their own or try to sound as learned as possible. It's an awkward situation, but I know it's only human nature at work. We'd all like to think that we are the smartest person in the room even if we know it's not true.

If given a choice to spend a week quarantined with really smart people or people of average intelligence, the average Jane would choose people of average intelligence. Who can blame her? But what a tragedy! It's as if Jane's fear, ego, or yearning to fit in prevents her from growing and learning. Overcoming this feeling of insecurity is the first step to ascending to greatness.

When in high school, I learned the value of hanging around brilliant people. Somehow I ended up befriending some really bright students. I make it sound coincidental, but the relationships I developed were probably strong because I was a social outcast, too, like they were. The geeks always are, right? Nevertheless, the end result was the same; I was able to learn so much from them and therefore increase my abilities. For example, in 1996, we were building dynamic websites for interactive presentations in class. Also, we were using programs to exchange data via our infrared ports on our Hewlett Packard scientific calculators. (And no, we didn't use the program to cheat!) We were ahead of our times in many ways. Many of my friends went on to Harvard, MIT, and other great schools.

Today, I continue to maintain an ever-expanding circle of intelligent people. My circle includes longtime CEOs, technologists, investors, and others, many of whom come from the top universities and companies in the world. They make me feel inadequate and sometimes just really stupid, but I am OK with that because I know that I learn so much from them. It's not easy to find and to develop solid relationships with smart people, especially as you grow older, but it's worth the effort.

Several quotations eloquently convey my point. For example, business philosopher and author E. James Rohn says, "You are the average of the five people you spend the most time with." I especially like this quotation because it incorporates mathematics, and it forces you to think about who those five people are. Likewise, this quotation is popular in Spanish-speaking countries: "*Dime con quién andas y te diré quién eres.*" Roughly translated, it means, "Tell me who you associate with, and I'll tell you who you are." As these quotations imply, we cannot help but pick up the habits and thoughts of those around us. Therefore, it behooves every entrepreneur—and anyone else who strives for success—to be surrounded with the brightest and best minds.

39) Office Space Is Not a Priority, But a Good Team Is

I think, team first. It allows me to succeed, it allows my team to succeed.
—LeBron James, NBA champion

One of the most costly mistakes I have made as an entrepreneur is to rent high-end office space, thinking that it would foster growth through increased productivity and project a more professional image. It did none of these. In fact, all it did was increase operating expenses and precipitate a drop in profits.

My company's culture started out quite differently from that of a traditional corporation, yet I felt the need to emulate a more corporate culture. Boy, was I wrong! As any veteran entrepreneur will tell you, the culture you start with will probably be the culture you end up with. Trying to get employees and staff to adopt a more rigid culture after years of having a relaxed culture is quite difficult. I learned the hard way. I ignored the fact that my staff enjoyed their flexibility and start-up identity. They resented the idea of having to come to the office at new mandatory times to do their work. Most of them worked for me because they were excellent team members and didn't need supervision or micromanagement. They were motivated to perform and to deliver in large part because of the flexibility our company afforded them. And they believed in what we were doing.

After the move to the new, plush office and the change to the culture, many employees became less productive. For instance, workers who were normally great in the morning now had morning commutes. Some of their commutes were one hour each way. Consequently, reports and important documents would arrive later in the day. Also, our meeting schedules changed, as we now adjusted times to accommodate traffic patterns. Based on what we were used to, the scheduling became a bit ridiculous. These are just a few changes that caused productivity to drop and anxiety to increase.

I also thought that having a nice office would project a more professional image and attract more prestigious clients. That didn't necessarily happen either. While clients would compliment our wonderful facilities and impressive skyline views of Buckhead, they were still most concerned with the quality of our products and services. Ultimately, that was most important to them.

Nowadays, having an office seems to be out of style. Not only is it not cool, but it is not smart in a slow economy if you don't need it. Because of this trend, there are now so many virtual office options. Regus, one of the largest of these virtual companies, gives you several options, ranging from a traditional corporate office to a mere mailbox with a physical address. A customer of Regus can have a physical address in over 1,500 different locations around the world; some of these addresses are quite prestigious. You can also have someone answer your calls or your staff's calls and route them to wherever you want. In other words, you can give the impression of having a full-fledged, multinational company when in fact you just have a clever façade.

Acquiring office space should always be justified by how it will improve your business and raise your profits. Office space is a luxury, not a necessity. I suggest that you adequately weigh the pros and cons. Most entrepreneurs, especially new ones, find more cons than pros. Save the money you would invest in office space to finance things that get you a solid return. Certainly, don't do what I did and jeopardize losing a great team to simply upgrade an office.

40) What You Wear Isn't What You're Worth

Clothes don't make the man.
—Unknown

Apparently, Wall Street investors prefer that disruption be applied to business and not to fashion.

When Mark Zuckerberg, cofounder of Facebook, began his IPO tour to persuade Wall Street investors to purchase stock in his company, he showed up in his iconic hoodie. In doing so, he continued a tradition of technology CEOs who shun formality, especially when it comes to dress. That's right, no million-dollar R. Jewels Diamond suit for Zuckerberg, whose über-casual garb often shocks the stodgy business types.

Interestingly, Zuckerberg's alleged lack of fashion sense was perceived as a not-so-subtle slight to the New York City financial world, where a Brooks Brothers suit and a Rolex are the acceptable uniform and "successory." Analysts were all agog. In fact, Wedbush's managing director Michael Pachter, an analyst, commented, "I'm not sure [Zuckerberg] is the right guy to run a corporation." He also said,

> Mark and his signature hoodie: He's actually showing investors he doesn't care that much; he's going to be him. I think that's a mark of immaturity. I think that he has to realize he's bringing investors in as a new constituency right now, and I think he's got to show them the respect that they deserve because he's asking them for their money.

These senseless comments, in addition to causing a whirlwind of backlash from the Silicon Valley faction and its casually clothed followers, affirm a basic point that I have always believed: Your worth should be a function of your aptitude, not your apparel. People like Pachter believe that the clothes make the man. This notion is ludicrous, and Zuckerberg, whose company at the time was worth nearly $100 billion, is the living antithesis of this corporate canon. Perhaps Pachter should try wearing a hoodie, so that he can loosen up and focus on what really matters—respecting the money and the man who generated it.

When it comes to what is acceptable to wear when doing business, conventional wisdom demands that you dress to impress, that you project the most professional image. However, my experience has been that the "suits," as they are affectionately known in Silicon Valley, are no more substantive than the "hoodies." In fact, the hoodies are often less concerned with social norms and more concerned about developing the best product possible or monetizing their inventions.

Don't get me wrong. I am not condoning that you dress to the point of being offensive. For example, when his company was young, Steve Jobs, the cofounder of Apple, was notorious for his counterculture dress, long hair, and body odor (only to be outdone in his mature years by a black turtleneck, loose-fit jeans, and running shoes). His coworkers constantly complained that he smelled bad because of his vegan diet and that he would begin picking at his feet during important meetings. Now that's just bizarre no matter how much of a genius you are.

Without going beyond the extremes of ridiculousness, wear what is comfortable to you to perform your best. Respectable and comfortable are not mutually exclusive. If a person cannot see past the irrelevancy of your clothing to assess the relevancy of your idea, perhaps you should move on. Cultural norms are changing for the better such that ideas are more important than if you're wearing Izod.

Ironically, Zuckerberg's bold move to wear a hoodie during his IPO road show says much more about his confidence than if he were to don the most expensive designer suit in the world. Besides, he owns a majority of his company, so what we think about what he wears doesn't really matter, and that supports what I have always believed. Beyond the patina of pretense that is fashion, there exists something much more important: the value of your ideas. The reality is that with or without a hoodie Mark Zuckerberg is still worth billions of dollars. That should be the end of discussion.

During Facebook's historic IPO, I got my wish: Zuckerberg wore a hoodie and sandals when he rang in the bell on the first day of trading for his company. I wasn't surprised. (Let's not forget that his business card reads, "I'm CEO, bitch.") That monumental dress-down day was the ultimate proof that what you wear isn't what you're worth.

41) You Don't Always Have to Be the Smartest One in the Room

You never really learn much from hearing yourself speak.
—George Clooney, actor, director

Have you ever listened to a CEO of a major company speak and wonder how in the world that person got to be CEO? Perhaps this "imposter" is not very articulate at all, or has no clue about the company and seems to be more like a figurehead than a deserving CEO. I think we all have experienced this scenario at one time or another.

When sizing up CEOs, we often make a huge mistake of trying to fit them into a box. There are so many stereotypes of what a CEO of a certain company should be like. For instance, a cool tech start-up should have a spindly, baby-faced young male who wears a hoodie and flip-flops. He speaks passionately and is knowledgeable, but his cadence is robotic. On the other hand, a financial services company should have an athletic, well-groomed male who wears an expensive suit with highly polished shoes. He is confident and charming. I could go on, but you get the idea. Whenever a CEO doesn't fit nicely into our stereotype, we automatically question the company.

The reality is that CEOs come in all different forms, and more often than not we are unable to fully witness all the talents of a CEO, especially if she is only speaking on a panel. Not every CEO is like Steve Jobs, who seemed to have it all—from piercing intelligence to amazing intuition. (We'll forget about the turtlenecks and temper tantrums for the moment.) Some CEOs are brilliant technologists. Others are great managers and know how to bring the best out of their people, and some CEOs are just great visionaries. As I matured as an entrepreneur, I learned to respect all types equally, but there was one experience I had at a young age that enabled me to begin to really appreciate the variety and its value.

Shortly after I decided to become an entrepreneur and started my first company, I attended a panel with a highly respected and venerated CEO in Atlanta. This CEO was a legend. Because of his larger-than-life reputation and tremendous success, I expected him to be the quintessential CEO. You know: charming, tall, and teeming with confidence. He was the complete opposite. In fact, I couldn't help but feel sorry for the man at times during his interview, because he could barely form a basic sentence with subject and verb. It was extremely difficult to follow him. Boy, was I in for a surprise, though. Despite my initial disappointment and difficulty in understanding him, I learned one of the biggest lessons I've learned during my several years as an entrepreneur. Toward the end of the panel, he looked at the large audience and said while stuttering, "I may not be the best speaker or the most articulate, but I know how to put together the right people. And I don't have to be the smartest person in the room all the time."

His final comment was so powerful and sums up my point. That evening, I learned that the most successful CEOs are the most humble. They know that they don't have all the answers; they know that they need help. If you are one of those entrepreneurs full of bravado who knows everything and is unwilling to listen to and to hire others, especially those smarter than you, you'll only get so far. The best entrepreneurs don't always have to be the smartest one in the room. They know better.

42) Talent Trumps Seniority

I'd rather have a lot of talent and a little experience than a lot of experience and a little talent.
—John Wooden, American basketball coach

The tension in the office was high. A burly senior developer looked my manager right in the eyes and shouted, "Don't ever ask an intern to develop an application without my approval! I don't care how good he is!" I was the intern in question.

My manager, who was quite bold, remonstrated, "Kevin said he could do it, and I've been asking you to do it for months. I thought it would be helpful." Seated behind his desk and irritated red, the senior developer asked me to leave his top-floor office while he continued to berate my manager. As the door shut behind me and I descended to my cubicle, a shouting match ensued. I wondered if I would be fired, but I decided right then and there that I would not give this bully the luxury of firing me. A few days later, I left the media company on my own terms, disgusted with what I had experienced.

About a week before this eye-opening meeting, my manager had asked me to create an application to track employee arrivals and departures. She mentioned that she really needed this application and that her boss was dragging his feet on producing it. Naturally I felt obligated to meet my manager's request. I told her that I could do the program and that it would take a few weeks to complete. She got excited that I had the technical knowledge to do it. I finished designing and coding the application that weekend and showed it to her the following week. Elated, my manager decided to show my program to the senior developer whom she originally asked to do the application. It was a bad idea for her and an awakening for me.

I woke up with the understanding that it makes no sense for a company to stifle the growth of its extraordinary young talent, giving favor to its senior people or a counterproductive protocol. That happens often in corporate environments. This type of culture ultimately leads to a company's demise or mediocrity. Conversely, companies led by young adults typically eschew the idea of special treatment because of seniority. Instead, they focus on merit and the ability to deliver results. For this reason, a majority of trailblazing companies with innovative ideas don't have many employees over the age of thirty and implement a flat organization.

It's not so much a secret anymore, but an expectation: Start-up tech companies prefer to hire people under thirty years old to avoid dealing with outdated and ineffectual norms that give preference to older people. For example, when Facebook started, it intentionally avoided hiring people in their late twenties and early thirties. Not until the company began to mature and needed to bring in experienced executives did it relax this practice. According to a recent book published about Facebook, the average age of the company's fourteen-hundred-plus employees was thirty-one in 2010. Similarly, PayPal during its early days had a young staff. In fact, Peter Thiel, the CEO of PayPal, was thirty-five at the time the company was sold to eBay. He was an elder member of the company.

Entrepreneurs believe that talent trumps seniority. Of course, I don't condone ageism. I do, however, advocate building an organization that promotes great results and not people for arbitrary reasons. If you want to win the game, don't bench your best players.

43) You Are Odd, and It's OK

Eventually, the nerds and the geeks will have their day.
—Judd Apatow, film producer, comedy writer

Chances are that when you think of the most successful and wealthy entrepreneurs, you don't think of a group of weird people. Instead, you probably think of well-respected and brilliant people who exhibit all the admirable qualities of well-rounded, well-adjusted leaders. Ironically, research shows just the opposite; entrepreneurs, especially those in technology, are indeed quite odd. In fact, the data show that being odd is the norm.

A recent survey of entrepreneurs conducted by Julie Login of Cass Business School found that 35 percent of those surveyed suffered from dyslexia, compared with 10 percent of the population as a whole. One reason for this trend posits that those with dyslexia, a learning disability affecting one's reading and comprehension, tend to delegate tasks to manage their disability. Some of the most notable dyslexics of our time are founders Steve Jobs of Apple, John Chambers of Cisco, and Richard Branson of the Virgin Group.

In another study, attention-deficit disorder (ADD) is common among entrepreneurs. A recent article in *The Economist* mentioned that "people with ADD are six times more likely than average to end up running their own businesses." Sufferers of ADD are known to be disorganized procrastinators who are unable to focus, all normally bad characteristics. But some entrepreneurs who have the disorder—like Paul Orfalea, founder of Kinko's—interpret these characteristics as an advantage because people with ADD can be creative in ways that "normal" people would not.

Furthermore, many entrepreneurs display symptoms of Asperger's syndrome, which, according to the Mayo Clinic, is a "developmental disorder that affects a person's ability to socialize and communicate effectively with others." Some refer to it as a mild form of autism. Asperger's is perhaps the most prevalent among software developers like me who would prefer to send an e-mail or instant message to someone sitting next to them in the office rather than to talk to them face to face. We often appear robotic and detached. Mark Zuckerberg, the cofounder of Facebook, is a good example of an entrepreneur who exhibits these traits. In Silicon Valley, several entrepreneurs display the symptoms of Asperger's syndrome. In fact, it's cool to act this way. Most people would just call it being a geek. In the Valley, the social butterflies are considered offbeat.

In addition to these disabilities, disorders, and syndromes, entrepreneurs have habits that are just plain bizarre. Steve Jobs had perhaps the strangest habits, including use of acid and LSD. In fact, he attributed his creativity to his taking LSD. Other CEOs have been said to perform karaoke in drag, to have an obsession with guessing measurements, to ideate underwater, and to wear the same clothing every day.

In a strange turn of events, these so-called oddities that are common among prominent entrepreneurs are attracting investors. To use a term in computer science, pattern matching has become quite popular. For instance, if you are looking for the next Facebook and you have to choose between funding two CEOs of equally great tech companies, one who is jovial and the other who is introverted, you'll probably go with the introvert. This may seem a bit ridiculous, but it happens more and more often.

So when it comes to being a successful entrepreneur, it pays to be odd. And besides, when you become wealthy and successful, people tend to forget how odd you might really be. Regardless, everyone wants to be your friend.

44) People Don't Only Work for Money

Do not hire a man who does your work for money, but him who does it for love of it.
—Henry David Thoreau, author, philosopher

I had it all wrong. I made a rookie mistake, but fortunately was able to correct it quickly.

When I started my third business, a college magazine, I had no knowledge of the publishing industry. I just knew that several major companies were willing to pay me as much as $6,000 for a full-page advertisement. It only cost me about $2,600 to produce the magazine. I planned to allocate about sixteen pages in the first issue to ads. I did the math and determined that with profit margins so potentially high, I would learn while on the job.

Neither did I know about the huge amount of work needed to produce a high-quality magazine. Thinking that the magazine could be published rather quickly, I set a launch date for one month after I decided to go into the publishing business and announced the date to the public. The month leading up to the official launch was one of the most stressful times I can remember. My small team and I worked hard.

To make a long story short, the magazine launched on time, and it was a huge success with readers. It was a great feeling to walk around campus and see students reading my magazine by the thousands. However, the huge profits I estimated before launch didn't materialize immediately. It took a few years for that to happen. The profits were low because my payroll was too high.

When I started the magazine, I thought that paying my staff was the honorable and logical thing to do, as if I were a fully developed enterprise. I didn't expect the students to work for free. Why should they? I assumed that they would work with me because they would appreciate the extra spending money. I was wrong.

As the magazine grew in popularity, we had more writers inquiring about positions. I had reached my budgetary limit but decided to let some writers work for free. Ironically, the writers who worked for free were often better than those we paid. It didn't take long for me to make an adjustment. I eventually learned that the student writers didn't care about money. They had enough spending money from Mom and Dad. Instead, they wanted the experience, college credit, and most importantly, college clout. As writers for the hottest publication on campus, they instantly became influencers. This influence was especially appealing to underclassmen.

Before long, I wasn't negotiating or even mentioning payment with writers anymore. Instead, I was negotiating perks like backstage passes to concerts, class credit, a chance to interview Janet

Jackson, a trip to MTV's Spring Break, or a stellar job recommendation. I leveraged the magazine and the many perks that came with it to recruit top talent.

Through this experience I learned that people are willing to work for things other than money. In fact, some people actually work harder when they don't get paid. If you can find what makes them tick or align your goals with their passions, you place yourself in a perfect position to draft them and keep them on your team. I mistakenly believed that because I was young and inexperienced, there was nothing I could offer them of value other than money. I was dead wrong and literally paid a price for it.

Before determining what you will pay people for their services, stop and think about what you can offer them instead of monetary compensation. Chances are you have something that they want, and you can use that as leverage.

45) You Have a Sidekick

Two heads are better than one.
—John Heywood, English playwright

One of my favorite events in the Summer Olympic Games is the 4×100 meter relay. In this event, a team runs 400 meters total, once around a regulation athletics track, with four teammates running 100 meters each. Currently, Jamaica holds the world record time of 36.84 seconds, achieved at the 2012 London Olympics. That Jamaican team included Usain Bolt, the fastest man and perhaps the most pompous athlete in the world. With teeming swagger and silly showmanship, he smashed the 100-meter dash record with an amazing time of 9.58 seconds in 2009. The three other runners on the winning relay team are world-class, too. The Jamaican team is always a favorite to break a relay record at the Olympic Games.

The 400 meters is another favorite event of mine. However, in this race only one athlete runs 400 meters, the same distance as the

4×100 meter relay. The world record in the 400 meters is held by the great Michael Johnson of the United States. Johnson ran 43.18 seconds in 1999. His record still stands almost thirteen years later. Despite this amazing accomplishment, his time is a huge 6.34 seconds slower than the 4×100 meter relay record. In track and field sprinting events, that difference is an eternity.

What does track and field have to do with entrepreneurship? The comparison of the times of these two races, one run by a single person and the other run by four teammates, perfectly explains why some companies excel and others lag far behind. The metaphor can even be extended to compare training regimens, options during injury, and race-day strategies. If you are an entrepreneur doing everything by yourself, you are competing against a world-class team of sprinters. Chances are you will be left behind, eating the dust of your competitors.

Young entrepreneurs often underestimate the productivity and efficiency of a team. Mesmerized by the possibility of making a lot of money, they believe that team members or cofounders would dilute their equity. This may be true, but the unfortunate assumption that usually accompanies this thinking is that the results would be the same—that a person working alone can produce as much as a team. That is unlikely with the right partners, and we all know that it is wiser to have 50 percent equity in a large company than 100 percent equity in a small company. Also, many young entrepreneurs prefer to avoid the dynamics and complications that come with having team members or cofounders. The value of adding another person to your team, however, supersedes these perceived hindrances.

Over the last twelve years of being an entrepreneur, I have seen such selfish and self-defeating attitudes cripple many founders. So many companies with great ideas are straggling along or dying out because of their founder's unwillingness to collaborate. These self-absorbed leaders are comfortable with coming in last place, a whopping "6.14 seconds" behind the winning team.

Looking at the greatest start-ups in history, you almost always see a teammate or cofounder from the beginning. Consider Google (Sergey Brin and Larry Page), Microsoft (Bill Gates and Paul Allen), Apple (Steve Jobs and Steve Wozniak), and Facebook (Mark Zuckerberg and Eduardo Saverin). These pioneers got it right. They realized that their chances of accomplishing their goals were greatly enhanced by the contributions of their teammate.

My most successful ventures have always been those in which I had great teammates. While creating one of the first online content management systems, OmniPublisher, my partner and I worked together like the parts of a new jet engine. Once he joined the project, productivity increased fourfold. Also, he brought a different and brilliant perspective to the table about business decisions and software production. His involvement also made the experience so much more fun.

The idea of one person running a race against four others seems a bit ridiculous, but so many entrepreneurs do exactly that. For whatever reason—pride, fear, or greed—they think they can win by themselves. Avoid this trap. If you don't have a team member or a cofounder, search for one. It may take some time and effort to find the right people, but once you do, you increase your chances for success greatly.

46) Don't Let People Abuse Your Flexibility

Work is hard. Distractions are plentiful. And time is short.
—Adam Hochschild, author, journalist

Being an entrepreneur is great, but it has its downside, too. One of the unfortunate realities that many entrepreneurs deal with is people's tendency to abuse their flexibility. This is especially true for entrepreneurs in strong relationships, ranging from friendships to marriages.

What do I mean by "abuse their flexibility"? I'll give you a recent example. My wife's car needed some repairs recently, so naturally she asked me to help her facilitate a speedy repair. Something told me that this was going to turn into a long ordeal, because we couldn't reproduce the car's problem at the dealership when we arrived. We had to go back and forth between home and the dealership to no avail. We finally decided to repair what we and our technician thought would fix the problem. To make a long story short, it took us four days to get the car fixed. In the meantime, I took my wife where she needed to go for work and for leisure. I must admit that after the second day, I became a bit frustrated because I had important work to do, and if I had a regular 9-to-5 job, my availability would have been severely limited. In that case, she would have been forced to respect my time. However, considering that I was not on the clock for anyone, *my* time was flexible.

Don't get me wrong. I love being able to help my wife, and I would make a hundred more trips to the dealership if I had to, but sometimes I feel like I am being held hostage. In other words, I feel like my flexibility is sometimes abused, like I have to pay the entrepreneur's flexibility tax. Furthermore, there's the guilt. What a cruel husband I would be if I said to my wife, "You know, honey, I am really sorry, but I am only available after five o'clock today, which means we cannot get your car repaired until the weekend." This would never pass, especially if I chose to work from home at any time during the week. The connubial eye would check in on me from time to time, evaluating the importance of everything I was doing. I dare not get caught on Facebook or Twitter during a quick break from "important" work.

While this situation is amplified in marriages, it shows up in friendships and other relationships, too. But regardless of whom the demanding person is, boundaries must be set and respected, even if it means hurting someone's feelings.

How do you set boundaries? Well, I wish I knew the answer myself. I suppose it differs depending on the strength and relevance of the relationship. Individual idiosyncrasies are certainly a factor, too. I suggest being frank with people who are taking advantage of your flexibility and telling them that you have work that must be done. Perhaps you can work out a deal. For instance, if your friend lets you get your work done, then you'll buy dinner and a movie. The right deal can make everyone happy.

I know it's easier said than done, but forcing people to respect your time and flexibility is only fair. Otherwise, you will always be on call. People who aren't entrepreneurs must learn that entrepreneurs are flexible because they work hard for that privilege. When that privilege is abused or at least not respected, frustration and angst ensue.

47) Don't Manage People, Manage Expectations

> High expectations are the key to everything.
> —Sam Walton, founder, Walmart

I am probably one of the worst managers ever. Perhaps I can blame an introverted personality that prefers to deal with computers rather than with people. (Computers don't need motivation or blame their kids for missing deadlines.) I realized that I had management shortcomings after I started my company, but this realization didn't come right away.

During the first three years operating my company, I didn't have a problem managing people. In fact, I don't even think I managed anyone but myself during that period. Everyone who joined my company in the first few years didn't receive any pay. They simply shared the vision for building the best web-based publishing software possible and worked diligently to make this a reality. These individuals, most of whom were technical like me, didn't need much management. There was an unspoken commitment and dedication to a tireless work ethic and the high expectations that we shared. There was no need to pull out the latest and greatest management software and begin managing anyone in the traditional sense. We really didn't have time for all of that, even if we wanted to do it.

However, I ran into problems when I began to hire people who weren't interested in the idea and team as much as they were eager to receive a paycheck. Bringing in people who didn't share the same motivations created a new headache that I wasn't prepared to endure. For example, I hired a graphic designer who was habitually late and who always had an excuse ready for me. He was much older than I was, so he came with a bevy of excuses that I didn't know how to handle. He would blame his wife, his kids, his jalopy—everything. Until I found the courage to tell him that I didn't care about those things, I let him get away with missing deadlines and slowing down the team's production. It was an especially frustrating time, but soon I had an epiphany.

I realized that you cannot manage people, only expectations. Conflict often comes from failed expectations. My relationship with the graphic designer was a prime example of this principle. Instead of giving the designer clear expectations to meet and communicating the consequences if these expectations were not respected, I treated him like my colleagues who didn't need what I called babysitting. That had to change.

Consequently, I put in writing, in painstaking detail, what the company and team required from him. He signed the document. From that point on, if he delivered designs late, I would refer to the document of expectations that he signed. There was no excuse that trumped the expectations to which he himself agreed. It was a powerful management tool.

I eventually had to let the graphic designer go. Although he did great work, he rarely met deadlines, and his personality and work ethic didn't fit the team's. In fact, he had a negative effect on our team's morale.

I learned a valuable lesson dealing with him and other unruly employees: Make sure that you don't try to manage people, because it's impossible. If you try to do that, you'll drive yourself crazy. Instead, define and manage expectations of individuals who work with you or for you. Clearly setting expectations in the beginning of the relationship and holding people to them avoids confusion and misunderstanding later. If you do this, you are on your way to becoming a much better manager than I was when I started my company.

48) Get the Right Mentor

Everybody can tell you how to do it, they never did it.
—Jay-Z, recording artist, entrepreneur

Since I started my business, I have been fortunate to have excellent mentors who have helped me to grow as an entrepreneur. In fact, not only have they been great advisers, but they have also brought me valuable clients. Without their counsel and referrals, I certainly would have made many more mistakes and had fewer clients.

The need for and benefits of mentors are well understood. I won't belabor the point. However, what's not so obvious is the type of mentors you should have and how often you should use them.

When you choose a mentor, be sure that the mentor has attained the level of success that you wish to reach. Align yourself with mentors who not only understand where you want to go but who also have been there. If you don't have at least one mentor who fits this role, you run the risk of receiving advice that actually stunts your growth or inhibits your vision. Often, a mentor's advice is limited by that person's experiences. For example, if you need to raise money via an angel investor or a venture capitalist, having a mentor who has been through this experience increases your chances of a successful capital campaign. Likewise, if your company has the potential to go public, you must have an adviser who understands what it takes to go through an initial public offering. An inexperienced mentor in these areas, even with the best intentions, may advocate that you bootstrap your company and avoid IPO dreams. Assuming that your company has blue-chip potential, this advice would be a disservice to your company.

Also, many entrepreneurs don't use their mentors enough. Whether entrepreneurs fear being a pest or don't understand the value of an additional opinion, they only use their mentors once in a while. But if you are working diligently on your business, you should be in constant contact with your mentor. Consult with your mentor on at least a monthly basis. I frequently shoot my mentor an e-mail about an issue or ask him if I can call and get his opinion on something. I promise him that the conversation will take no more than five or ten minutes, and I do my best to stick to that time limit. If I go over, I ask for permission to continue. I want to be respectful of his time and willingness to help me.

Many entrepreneurs have quarterly advisory board meetings. That's fine, but they should not take the place of a more personal and impromptu relationship. Boards are important, but I recommend that you have at least one mentor who is on call and who can answer your questions on the day that you ask them.

No entrepreneur has succeeded without some type of mentor figure. Mentors are invaluable. Make sure that the one you choose has achieved what you want and that you consult that mentor frequently. If your mentor is not accomplished enough or is inaccessible, find someone else who can really help you move closer to achieving your goals.

49) Choose Your Spouse Wisely

The most important career choice you'll make is who you marry.
—Sheryl Sandberg, COO, Facebook

As I watched my life play out on the big screen in the movie *The Social Network*, I smiled, reminiscing about my college days when I, too, was an instant campus superstar like Mark Zuckerberg, cofounder of Facebook. It was a defining moment in my life.

Just like Zuckerberg in the movie, I was a geeky computer science major with a handful of brainiac friends; then suddenly I was "the man" with more friends than I could have ever imagined. I had created a popular, online community for college students, complete with a dynamic book exchange, a dating service, chat rooms, news, photo galleries, and other neat features. Naturally, with my newfound fame came the groupies, the women who didn't necessarily have an interest in me as much as my ability to rub elbows with moguls like P. Diddy and Kanye West.

Before long, I had my first serious girlfriend, a very demanding one who didn't take no for an answer. (Recall Eduardo's crazy girlfriend in the movie.) She didn't understand that I was a geek and that there was nothing more satisfying to me than coding a brilliant new feature for my website. In other words, she couldn't accept that she was a distant number three at best, just after PHP and mySQL (computer programming languages).

One night I knew things were going south—and fast. The hour was late. I was in my room working on the computer and in walked my girlfriend. She seductively sprawled on the edge of the bed, naked except for high heels and nylons. I barely noticed. She erupted with fury, screaming, "I don't need this. I could call some other guys in my black book." I didn't respond. I was too busy, already making love to my PC. I had an epiphany that climactic night; I realized just how much ground I had lost in building my company.

Fast-forward. She broke up with me. Simply put, she wanted sex, and I wanted success. Of course, both desires are not mutually exclusive, but the former surely can be a distraction—and in my case, that's exactly what it was. The fact that my college crush dumped me for being extremely focused was the best thing that happened to me at that moment.

After the breakup, I devoted myself 100 percent to growing my technology and media business. It paid off. Within weeks of implementing my monetization plan, I received my first check from a firm that purchased a banner ad for $1,800. Soon after, I partnered with a classmate and computer whiz. Together we created OmniPublisher, one of the first online content management applications. A few years later, I sold it to a publishing company.

Perhaps this story is a circuitous and somewhat inflated way to prove a basic point, but it is certainly a lesson that all young entrepreneurs must learn: Choose a mate who understands that your drive to succeed at times trumps satisfying their sex drive—among other things. Distractions in the form of bad or draining relationships have wrecked so many businesses. In fact, many venture capitalists devalue a company's worth based on the increased risk that married cofounders present. When choosing a mate, make sure that person is an asset, not a liability.

Epilogue: Last time I heard, my ex isn't doing so well. But things have turned out pretty well for me, as it relates to success and . . . you know. I married an awesome woman who loves my entrepreneurial focus and encourages me all the time.

50) Fire Unproductive People

Hire slow, fire fast.
—Unknown

I recently received a desperate call for help from one of my mentees, who is working hard to grow his new clothing company. He sought advice about how to deal with a lazy business partner who is preventing the company from moving forward. My mentee wrote,

I have been working on my company for the past few months and things are going OK. I have a friend who I have known since 1996. He is also working on our clothing line. He says that he is interested in combining our ideas and working together. . . . That was almost a year ago. At the beginning, he was eager and helping a lot. Now, not as much. There hasn't been much communication about what he wants to do. I questioned him last month to see what ideas he had. Basically, he just said that he is still thinking about ideas, but he's broke. I don't have much money either, but I have gotten shirts printed and ready to sell. At this point, I'm lost. It's like he says one thing and does something else. What do you think I should do? Should I try to work it out by myself or should I cut ties and find a business partner who is not a friend, but who is serious about things?

As soon as I finished reading his e-mail, I replied, "It sounds like you've already made a decision, a right decision. You don't have time to wait. Find someone who is on top of their game." I hope he takes my advice.

My mentee faced a common challenge for entrepreneurs: finding and keeping the best talent to accomplish their business goals. Other than financial problems, this challenge is probably the most nerve-wracking part of growing a business, especially if you have few resources to attract and compensate workers. Regardless of the situation, great entrepreneurs find the right people to make their dreams happen.

There are two types of entrepreneurs when it comes to finding talent.

One type of entrepreneur is weak and indecisive on personnel decisions. Such a person is desperate to find a business partner, contractor, or employee, accepting practically anyone without the proper due diligence. Lacking the patience or knowledge to screen people, this type of entrepreneur is quick to enlist a friend or acquaintance and slow to fully assess a prospect's worth. A person whose performance is poor or hurting the business receives multiple second chances. Finally, the entrepreneur is too scared to pull the trigger and perhaps fire the least productive people on the team. The firing comes eventually, after valuable time and resources have been wasted.

The other type of entrepreneur is strong and resolved, ruthless in pursuit of good people and committed to finding good team members. There's no rush to judgment about prospects; those who eventually join the team are the best people for the job. Decisions come without emotion, and nepotism is never an option. Poor performers rarely get second chances. This type of entrepreneur reaches goals more quickly because of thorough, wise, and fair personnel decisions. Every entrepreneur should follow this model.

One of the biggest misconceptions about forming a team or hiring employees is that once you find great people, your personnel problems are solved and that everyone will constitute a tight and effective unit for years to come. Business rarely works out that way, especially for young companies. For reasons ranging from poor performance to recruitment by other companies, you can expect to lose people. Because attrition is inevitable, entrepreneurs and leaders of small companies must be committed to *always* looking for good talent.

Accept only the best people for your business. If you are most efficient in your search for talent, even the lesser candidates you consider will be above average. As a result, your company will grow faster and last longer.

Chapter 4

Finance

Money isn't the most important thing in life, but it's reasonably
close to oxygen on the "gotta have it" scale.
—Zig Ziglar, author, motivational speaker

Though it sounds obvious, this basic idea must be emphasized from time to time: You are in business to make
money. Caught up in the throes of everyday business activities, ranging from selling to managing operations, entrepreneurs
often leave matters of finance to fall by the wayside. By the time
they realize the importance of closely monitoring their finances, it
is too late; the damage has been done.

This chapter presents different ways to stay on top of your personal and business finances to avoid problems. Moreover, you'll
find advice on how to secure investment funds for your company.
You don't have to become a guru of cash flow analyses and balance sheets, but you do need to understand some basic concepts.

---

51) You Don't Need Money to Make Money

Money won't create success, the freedom to make it will.
—Nelson Mandela, former president, South Africa

Nothing is more irritating than hearing one of the many generalizations that permeate the business world and corrupt the minds of new entrepreneurs. You've heard them. You may even deal in these false aphorisms: "Follow your passion." "Fake it 'til you make it." "Entrepreneurs are born, not made." However, perhaps the most damaging to new entrepreneurs is the following: "It takes money to make money." No statement is more wrong or misleading.

I vividly remember when, where, and from whom I first heard this phrase. I was barely in my twenties and in downtown Atlanta, meeting with an accomplished entrepreneur who owned her own graphic design studio. I don't remember the context of our conversation, but when she said those six words I was perplexed. I was more impressed with the phrasing itself than its validity. At that point, I had started my first three companies with hardly any money at all. What she said just didn't make sense and certainly wasn't applicable to me.

My first company, a website for college students, didn't require much money at all. If anything, it demanded only my time and computer programming skills. During the first few years of the business, I only spent money on web hosting and a domain name, although it certainly wasn't necessary. Those costs were about $30 monthly. My second company, which produced a web-based content management system, had similar, nominal costs. Finally, my third company, a magazine, didn't require money at all. I simply came up with the idea and went out to sell it before it existed. For each business, I assumed that raising money was not even an option, and I am glad that I did. Had I heard that awful phrase, I may have delayed or killed my ventures, thinking that I had to raise money. Instead, I figured it out and, most importantly, attacked my goal with the resources I had.

Having access to start-up capital when you don't need it can actually stunt your growth. What is intended to help can turn out to be quite harmful. For instance, you can burn through cash unnecessarily, buying products and services that you could otherwise figure out how to obtain free of charge. That money could be used to purchase more important things. I cringe when I see a young entrepreneur's start-up costs include items like office supplies and computers when they are absolutely unnecessary. These individuals don't have the right state of mind of seeking to save money whenever possible. Perhaps they heard and were influenced by the very phrase that I am attempting to refute.

Now that I have been in business for over a decade, I think the phrase—altered a little bit—can be applied to specific situations. I would rephrase it this way: "It often takes money to make a whole lot of money." As I raise money for my next start-up, the reality of this interpretation is all too real. When you aim to execute a big idea fast, an infusion of cash is necessary in many cases. To illustrate, most people would agree that the idea of starting a nuclear power plant with no money is ludicrous. In this case, before you have actual revenue, you would have to spend a significant amount of money. Regardless, most entrepreneurs do not raise capital to start their business.

Don't believe the hype about needing money to start a business. It's deceiving, and if you believe it, you could be ruining or delaying the success of your own endeavor. People who repeat such generalizations are sometimes simply trying to sound wise and learned, or they are trying to justify why they are broke.

Having no money doesn't mean you have no resources. You've got something, so get started on your new business—and without spending any money if you can.

52) Pay Taxes Quarterly

You don't pay taxes. They take taxes.
—Chris Rock, comedian, actor

I was anxious out of my wits as I sat in my chair waiting for the calculations to tabulate. I had dreaded this day ever since the previous January, when I knew I had only three months left until the deadline. On that early March day, my accountant hit the enter button on his keyboard with an accented motion and said nonchalantly without even looking at me, "You owe . . . " I heard the astronomical number that followed, but it didn't register as reality. I panicked inside, trying not to blurt out an expletive and bring unwanted attention to myself. What I had feared was actually happening. I owed the government more taxes than I could pay.

When I started my company, the only thing I knew about business taxes was that I had an EIN (Employee Identification Number) needed to open a bank account and that I would eventually have to pay corporate taxes. I had no idea how to plan for what I would need to pay annually in taxes, and frankly that was the last thing on my mind. I was more concerned with perfecting my product and trying to sell it. Likewise, when I started to make significant money, tax planning was not a priority. Because of my negligence, I ended up spending almost everything my company made to grow the business and to pay salaries. It was a novice mistake that I would literally pay for later.

If I could go back in time to give myself advice, I would have suggested that I search online (remember Altavista and Webcrawler?) for basic accounting information on corporate tax planning. I would have also advised myself to find an accountant who specialized in helping new businesses prepare for their impending tax obligations. Following this basic advice would have saved me the paralyzing stress of finding out that I was in over my head on tax day. Only a teenager when I started my company, I was terrified of what the IRS would do to me if I were delinquent. I thought IRS agents would arrest me, seize my possessions, and fine me at least $100 each day I was late paying them the money I owed.

Now that I am wiser and have an accountant who does more than crunch numbers for me before the annual corporate tax deadline of March 15, I have a plan to pay estimated taxes for my S corporation. Estimated taxes are based on your expected adjusted gross income, deductions, credits, and so on. According to the IRS website, "If you are filing as a sole proprietor, partner, S corporation shareholder, and/or a self-employed individual, you generally have to make estimated tax payments if you expect to owe tax of $1,000 or more when you file your return." Those who opt to pay estimated taxes are required by the IRS to pay them quarterly. Following this method helps taxpayers avoid the sticker shock that I experienced the first time I owed the government a lot of money for taxes.

After receiving the bad news from my accountant years ago, I summoned my entrepreneurial creativity to figure out how I could earn money quickly to pay the tax bill. I came up with a plan and was able to pay what I owed on time. I learned my lesson well, and apparently I am not the only one. Over the years, I have heard similar stories from other entrepreneurial tyros. If you are just starting a company or already have one, don't be like us. Make sure that you pay estimated taxes quarterly to avoid being chopped by the tax ax.

53) A Check in Hand Means Nothing

Honesty is for the most part less profitable than dishonesty.
—Plato, Greek philosopher

If I had listened to my intuition, I could have saved myself some trouble. I would have heeded the many clues that the shoddy owners of the mom-and-pop business gave me. I would have run out of their dubious restaurant as fast as I could and never come back.

Instead, I ignored my intuition and accepted the restaurant's order to place an advertisement in my magazine. I told the owners, a wife-and-husband team, that our next issue was going to press soon and that they would see a quick return on their investment. I prepared the order, took their check, and ran their full-page, color ad.

The adventure and hard lesson began a few days later when I checked my bank account, which was off by $321, the exact amount I had charged the restaurant for its ad. After a closer look at my account's recent transactions, I noticed that the customer's check had bounced. Sure enough, a few days after that, I received the restaurant's rubber check in the mail with the damning NSF (nonsufficient funds) stamp, and my bank had charged me severe penalties for it. It was the first bounced check that I had ever received in my life, and I wasn't happy about it.

A completely naïve, young entrepreneur, I assumed that everyone who wrote a check had money in the bank to cover the amount. Apparently, I came from Pleasantville, the imaginary place where everything is perfect and everyone's word, or check in this case, is bond. The business world is nowhere near the utopian Pleasantville. No, there will always be people in business who try to take advantage of you, and that's exactly what these rogue restaurant owners did.

I shared my experience and frustration with my mentor. I told him that I wasn't so upset about the check bouncing as much as the owners probably knowing that they wrote a bad check. In his nonchalant tone, he admonished me, saying, "Simple solution: If you suspect that someone has given you a bad check, take that check to the bank written on the check and ask if there are sufficient funds in the account. A bank teller will tell you that information. If there is, you can cash the check right then and there." I was surprised to learn this. His solution would totally eliminate the risk associated with submitting a questionable check to my bank, which would charge me if the check was indeed bad. From that point on, I did just that for suspicious customers, and it has saved me similar trouble. I also learned that it is against the law to write bad checks.

I don't recall if I ever got my $321. I think I did after going to the customer's bank repeatedly until the funds were available. Regardless, I learned a valuable lesson that shapes my company's policy to this day: A check in hand means nothing. In other words, don't count your money until it's in the bank—and in there for a while.

When you receive a new purchase order, a check, a verbal agreement, or a written agreement from a customer wanting to buy your product or service, don't get too happy and excited. Save the celebration until you have cold cash in hand or the funds are verified.

54) Avoid Negative Cash Flow

To become successful you must learn how to manage cash flow.
—Robert T. Kiyosaki, author, *Rich Dad, Poor Dad*

I had no idea when I entered the media business that it was, as my mentor put it, "the easiest business to get into, but the hardest to stay in." After a few months into my venture, I learned the hard way exactly what he meant.

My challenge was cash flow. So many start-up businesses struggle with understanding and managing cash flow, which is simply a measure of a company's financial health. It equals cash receipts minus cash payments over a given period of time. Bad cash flow management is one of the main reasons start-ups go out of business in their first year, even if they are profitable. How does this happen? First let's look at an example dealing with personal expenses.

Many people manage cash flow every month as they struggle to pay bills and hope that they have money left over to save, buy a new car, or go on a nice vacation. If you have a job, you may know the feeling of having lots of bills that are due and anticipating payment from your employer so that you can pay those bills. At that moment in time, when you have bills due that same day and a payday two weeks away, you have a negative cash flow position. The reverse situation, when you have more money available than bills due that same day, is a positive cash flow position.

Businesses also struggle with managing cash flow. During the first year of publishing my magazine, enough advertising was sold to cover costs. We encouraged and incentivized prepayment for advertisements so that we could use that money to pay for printing, distribution, and other costs, but not all buyers were able to pay upfront. We extended some customers credit, giving them thirty days to pay us in full. When it was time to pay for our operating expenses, we had barely enough money to do so. Those customers to whom we extended credit normally paid in ninety days instead of thirty. We were profitable on paper, but could never quite get ahead of money going out the door to sustain operations. I was eventually able to get ahead, but doing so was difficult, especially since I had less available credit than I needed to float my operation while we collected receivables. Despite overcoming this problem, sometimes I felt like the end was near—such as when I had to print a new issue but still hadn't received money from advertisers in previous issues. It was not a good feeling at all.

Negative cash flow is not a bad thing per se. In fact, it is necessary for many businesses in numerous industries, particularly if the business is in the start-up phase. However, maintaining a negative cash flow position for too long is detrimental to any business. Your goal as leader should be to find out what the norms are for your industry and what is healthy. A financial adviser can also help you understand your options so that you can avoid this financial stumbling block.

Your company can be profitable but headed out of business, leaving you with a heap of debt and a feeling of despair. It happens every day to promising but poorly managed companies. For your business, ensure that you not only do monthly income statements but also monthly cash flow statements. As a result, you will better understand how to avoid a devastating, negative cash flow position, whether by decreasing expenses, tightening your sales cycle, or receiving a cash infusion. Ultimately, you can avoid a rude awakening and some start-up frustration.

55) Borrow Money from a Bank before You Need It

A bank is a place that will lend you money if you can prove that you don't need it.
—Bob Hope, comedian, actor

When Lehman Brothers filed for bankruptcy in fall 2008 signaling the start of the Great Recession, I had a clear premonition that things were going to get bad really fast.

The announcement of the collapse was especially untimely for me. During the same period that the investment bank's epic failure made national news, my wife and I were married. To remember our joyous union, we saved the newspaper from that beautiful fall day. The headline of the *Atlanta Journal-Constitution* read, "U.S. Tries Hands-On Bank Fix." The article stated, "The United States and the globe's other industrial powers pledged to take 'decisive action and use all available tools' to prevent a worldwide economic catastrophe." It was yet another harbinger of economic calamity, the proportions of which had not been seen since the Great Depression. I told my wife, "If the economy collapses, at least we have each other, honey!"

Likewise, the timing couldn't have been worse for my business. Almost immediately, the business environment deteriorated. Companies began to go into survival mode. Many of my best clients called to cancel orders. Companies that I had long-term relationships with severed ties. New prospects showed no interest in buying. Financial experts warned of the impending credit crunch. My company's cash flow position was getting worse everyday. I couldn't stand around and watch my company slowly die. I was desperate to save it, so I decided to explore all options, including getting a loan from a major bank.

Not expecting much, I consulted with one of my trusted bankers at Washington Mutual. She told me that I had no good options. Considering the recession and my poor cash position, no financial product available could help my company. She added that few businesses were receiving financing at the time. Hardly any credit lines were being extended. Likewise, hardly any installment loans were issued. The bank was open, but really it was closed.

With no reasonable options, I sourly remembered what an experienced banker had told me years before: "Borrow money from a bank before you need it." It made sense when I had heard his words, but I never followed his advice. I had waited too long, and here I was hoping that a bank would save my company when ironically the bank needed saving itself. (Washington Mutual was acquired by Chase a few months later.) Instead of relying on a cash infusion from a bank to help my company weather the economic storm, my team and I would have to survive the old-fashioned way by hitting the pavement and working harder than ever. I learned my lesson.

Banks prefer to lend to businesses that already have money and show signs of good financial health. Why? These businesses are most likely to pay back loans and thus are a low risk. On the other hand, distressed companies are a high risk and won't find many conventional loan products at a major bank. They must seek alternative financing that invariably carries higher interest rates. Sounds counterintuitive, but banks and many other lending institutions operate this way. In another example of reverse logic, few people know that banks consider deposits liabilities, not assets.

When your company is experiencing high growth and increased revenues, strengthen your capital structure. For example, apply for additional credit lines or request an extension of your current lines. Moreover, apply for an installment loan if appropriate to fuel more growth. Also, raise money from investors. As the economy shows small signs of recovery, banks are promoting new products and beginning to take greater risks. Take advantage of these opportunities.

Entrepreneurs must be mindful that recessions and economic downturns are inevitable. If you are in business long enough, you will experience one. Preparing your company to weather these storms is part of your job. One of the best ways to do this is to secure your company's financial welfare by applying for and receiving credit when you don't need it. If you wait until you need it, you could have the same fate as Lehman Brothers.

56) Prepayment Is King; Disregard Standard Payment Terms

Lack of money is the root of all evil.
—George Bernard Shaw, Irish playwright; cofounder, London School of Economics

Recent court documents reveal the cofounder of Facebook's frustration with a client who failed to pay him for his computer programming services in 2004. At the time, Mark Zuckerberg was still a computer science major at Harvard. He wrote in January 2004, "I contracted out my services for money, and even though I seem to continually be providing services, I don't seem to be receiving money from you guys." The client was a man named Paul Ceglia. Ceglia later replied in February, "I will do my best to try to raise the cash needed to pay the amount requested though I honestly cannot guarantee it." When this reply was sent, Ceglia owed Zuckerberg $10,000. Thefacebook was founded during the same month that these last e-mails were exchanged. In 2011, Ceglia sued Zuck-

erberg for a 50 percent stake in Facebook, claiming that Zuckerberg stole his idea. Ceglia eventually withdrew his case.

While some reports on this frivolous case focus on Zuckerberg's frustration, I immediately thought something different: *Why
was Zuckerberg doing work for a client and not getting paid? Isn't
this guy supposed to be really smart?* I was perplexed. Then I recalled that he nearly sold a company to Microsoft in high school
for about $1 million. Perhaps he thought the risk of not being paid
was low, and if the client didn't pay, he wouldn't be out of much
money, time, or effort. I tried to rationalize his response. I ultimately concluded, knowing from experience, that regardless of
what *he* thought then, it's never a good idea to do work with questionable payment arrangements or to continue work with a delinquent client.

New entrepreneurs often do work for clients who take advantage of them. I was one of them. I remember vividly how I
dealt with my first rogue client. Whereas Zuckerberg was twenty
years old during his dispute with Ceglia, I was twenty-two when I
had my dispute with a customer. I created software for a client who
was using it but not paying. I decided to sue him in small claims
court. The entire experience was a bit scary. Nevertheless, I went
to the courthouse in downtown Atlanta and filed my papers for
about $75. The client, who wasn't that much older than me, ended
up paying me the full amount he owed. Accompanied by his father,
he brought cash and paid me in the hall just before our case was
called. We informed the clerk that we had resolved the matter, and
the case was closed.

Since that experience, I have learned and adopted several strategies to ensure faster payment.

1. *Build trust immediately.* During the selling or price negotiation process, work hard to build trust so that you can ask for and
receive prepayment for services or a product. Give references before the client asks for them. Also, ensure that your brands and

work are presented in the most professional manner, so that the client feels comfortable paying upfront.

2. *Be clear with your payment terms*. Make sure that terms are well-defined for both sides from the very beginning—and in writing. Always present a clear and concise policy for payment terms, so that the client knows exactly what to expect and what you expect.

3. *Be aggressive with your timeline*. Ask for prepayment first, and then consider longer payment periods if necessary. Do whatever it takes to get paid on time. Don't be afraid to ask for what you want. Pick up the check in person, if you have to. In a perfect world, there is no such thing as net thirty days. I prefer net now.

The nature of business is that buyers want to pay as late as possible, and sellers want to be paid as early as possible. Your goal as an entrepreneur is to maintain good cash flow, and the best way to do that is to receive your money as soon as possible. You must be confident and direct about when you expect to be paid. Yes, it can be awkward and uncomfortable at times, but take it from Zuckerberg and me: it sure beats not being paid at all or having to go to court.

57) Hiring a Professional Accountant Is Money Well Spent

I have no use for bodyguards, but I have very specific use for two highly trained certified public accountants.
—Elvis Presley, singer, actor

Before I knew better, accountants were about as fun to visit as dentists. In fact, if you had asked me whether I wanted a dentist to fill my cavity or an accountant to do my tax return, I probably would have chosen dental work. My reasoning: Although the dentist would inflict more physical pain, at least his services would be cheaper than the accountant's. I was naïve and young then. Now I would most certainly prefer to visit my accountant.

When starting out, most entrepreneurs do everything they can to cut corners. That's understandable, because resources are low. They serve as the CEO, director of marketing, director of sales, mailroom clerk, custodian, and accountant all in one. During the early stages of a venture, no one wants to be wasteful, so the more tasks an entrepreneur assumes, the more money is saved—or so the thinking goes. This misconception, though, will not only drive you nuts to the point of burnout, but it will also cost you. Contrary to what Intuit would like you to believe, you don't save money keeping your own books. It's not worth the headache to be your own accountant.

During my first year as an entrepreneur, I quickly decided that trying to figure out how to be an accountant was not worth my time. I drove to the closest H&R Block and asked for help. An older gentleman, who reminded me of Arnold Palmer, helped me get on the right track. He was pricey, but I was glad to have him crunch numbers and save me the hassle. I stayed with him even when he left H&R Block to start his own practice in rural Georgia. I stopped going after the second year, when his new office was located in a dilapidated building, complete with bad wooden paneling, plastic dividers between dingy offices, and a questionable gun exchange. It's probably confabulation, but I think there was even a stuffed bear in the office, too. I had my limits, so I found a new guy who turned out to be cheaper and more knowledgeable.

Since then, I have had the same accountant for almost ten years. He's great. He does his work quickly, reminds me when forms and payments are due, gives me great advice, advocates on my behalf, and is highly accessible. Even better, his office is fairly new, and no dead animals are hanging from the wall. He saves me tens of thousands of dollars that I'd be wasting because of lack of knowledge. If I could convert time to money, that figure would be much higher.

If you are still not convinced that you should hire an accountant, ponder these three compelling reasons.

1. *Accountants save you money.* The money I spend having a professional accountant crunch numbers for me is much less than the money he saves me. During tax time, for example, I would probably miss some important deductions. America's tax code is highly complicated, and unless you are a professional, you are likely to misunderstand something or totally overlook an opportunity to keep more of your money. Say the accountant recommends a deduction that yields an annual savings of $500. Over the next ten years, I would save $5,000 that otherwise I would have paid out.

2. *Accountants save you time.* This is a no-brainer. As CEO of your company, you have better things to do than to reconcile expense sheets and issue 1099s. Your focus should be on growing your company. An accountant frees you from this burden and reduces your stress.

3. *Accountants are not that expensive.* To continue with our tax scenario, an accountant can charge from $400 to $800 to file a basic annual tax return. If that sounds like a lot, don't worry. I assure you that you will get that money back. Put to the test, any good accountant will pass it.

As an entrepreneur, you have to decide what services to pay for, and accounting is one of them. Although accounting services may seem expensive, especially if you are just starting out, I guarantee that you will save money in the end. From the very beginning, finding a good accountant is a high priority. Don't think of doing business without one.

58) Manage Debt Well

Rather go to bed without dinner than to rise in debt.
—Benjamin Franklin, entrepreneur; Founding Father, United
States of America

Years ago, when I was just out of college, I saw an ad in a local Atlanta newspaper that promoted a bank's new business line of credit product. Soon after, I thought I would apply for it. I stopped by the bank's closest branch, filled out the one-page application, and returned it to the banker, not knowing what to expect. In just a few minutes, the banker hung up the phone and told me the verdict. She looked at me with a big smile and said, "You were approved for $18,000." Just a few minutes later, I walked out of the bank with a business line of credit for $18,000. Combined with another business line and credit cards I received from other banks, I had about $45,000 to fund my next big idea. I was excited and horrified at the same time.

Growing up, I learned the importance of managing my personal finances well. My father, who often boasted of having "A1" credit, instilled in my siblings and me that a well-managed financial life is a good life. He worked in the credit department of a major retail store for decades, so discussing money and credit in our household was normal. I suppose he was determined to teach his kids how to avoid the bad financial situations that he witnessed daily at work. Specifically, he taught us to pay our bills on time—before the grace period—and to never incur more debt than we can pay back in a reasonable time. I never imagined that I would be leveraging credit in the tens of thousands of dollars to realize my business dreams. If I had asked my dad, he probably would have discouraged me from incurring so much debt at such a young age. It wouldn't have mattered; I was determined and ready to assume the risk. Luckily, my business idea was highly profitable, and I was able to service all debt that I assumed.

Research indicates that the great majority of entrepreneurs will never receive money from a venture capitalist or an angel investor. Instead, they will fund their businesses with their own money and via credit cards. According to a report by the National Federation of Independent Business, in 2009, 83 percent of businesses with fifty employees or fewer used credit cards. This point is important, because how you manage your personal finances determines how much money you can borrow for your business and at what interest rate. In my case, I received access to $45,000 in large part because my father helped me to build a solid credit history from a young age. When I applied for the business lines of credit and credit cards, I received a substantial amount of money at a competitive interest rate because my personal credit was good.

How one manages personal debt is a good indicator of how business debt will be managed. For that reason, banks and other creditors check your personal credit when assessing your credit-worthiness for a business loan product. Similarly, I often vet entrepreneurs by learning about their personal finances. Like the banks, I am less likely to invest in people who can't manage their own finances well, regardless of how great the idea or how large the profit margins.

Over the years I've learned that "debt" is not such a dirty word. You just have to know how to use it. I wasn't able to change my perspective until I began to conquer my debt. Currently, I have no car note, no student loans, and no credit card debt. Aside from my mortgage, I am debt free. Last time I checked, my FICO score was 813, in the top 10 percent. Likewise, my business maintains a healthy debt-to-income ratio, and all of our accounts are in good standing.

The best entrepreneurs manage their personal debt well. Also, they find the best money mentors or financial gurus to help put them in a position of maximum financial leverage. Undercapitalization continues to be the main reason so many businesses fail. Considering this, you want to ensure that you do everything you can to maximize your chances of success. Yes, it's important to have a good idea and eventually a profitable business, but following the right financial path to get there is critical, too.

59) There's a Downside to Having Investors

Angel investor funding (venture capital or private for that matter) for your business is a bad idea sometimes.
—Ryan Mapes, general manager, Go BIG

In the world of entrepreneurship, investors are like gods. Why else would the term "angel investor" exist? These omnipotent and mystical figures have tremendous power and influence, helping determine what companies will ultimately join them in the land of milk and honey. However, having investors is not always a heavenly experience. In fact, having investors can make your life a living hell, especially if you make some deadly assumptions about them and their purpose like so many entrepreneurs do.

As a young entrepreneur I committed this cardinal sin: I assumed that I needed outside investors to grow my company. Everything I read about entrepreneurship stressed the importance of having investors—and at an early stage. According to the books I read, only the most successful businesses had investors. If your idea isn't funded, then it's not legitimate or big enough, right? I don't remember many books discussing the idea of bootstrapping as a real option for a young start-up. If a book did mention this option, it provided little or no information on when or how bootstrapping should be used. In contrast, most books focused on less pragmatic methods of finding capital that most entrepreneurs will never need.

As a result of my assumption, I set out to learn everything I could about venture capitalists and the Holy Grail, an IPO (initial public offering). I bought *High-Tech Start-Up*, a phenomenal book by John L. Nesheim on creating successful new high-tech companies. The book thoroughly discussed the IPO process and the idio-syncrasies of venture capitalists, angel investors, and other types of investors. I was convinced that my idea was big enough for an IPO, so I studied the book like it was my Bible. I vividly remember studying the equity tables of Microsoft, Apple, DoubleClick, eBay, MP3.com, Oracle, and other companies provided in the book's appendix. I later learned that a great majority of businesses will never reach an IPO, and that according to Saratoga Venture Finance, the odds of going public are about six in a million.

Although my initial businesses were not IPO-worthy—far from it—I did eventually create fundable ideas that would need outside capital to grow and to scale. As I sought and received funding for some of these ideas, my assumptions about having investors eventually would cause me quite a bit of frustration. Three assumptions I had about outside investors are as follows:

1. *Finding investors will be easy.* Overcome by the excitement and conviction of their idea, most entrepreneurs assume that finding investors will be a walk in the park. It is not. I am reminded of Walt Disney's amazing story of perseverance when he sought capital to build his studios. It wasn't a walk in the "amusement" park for him. Disney was rejected by 302 banks! Most of us would have given up after the fifth bank's rejection. Moreover, finding investors isn't easy because it is energy-intensive. A good friend of mine, who recently raised capital for his technology company, was always on the road, meeting with different venture capitalists and angel groups. His travel schedule was grueling, not to mention the constant drilling by brilliant cynics who wanted to put holes in his business model. It takes the attitude of a marathoner to find capital for your business: When you want to give up, you dig deep to keep going.

2. *When you receive a yes from an investor, all your money problems will go away.* Not true. In many ways, your problems may be just starting. Rarely do you hear about investment deals going awry, but they often do. After appearing on the popular

show *Shark Tank*, contestant Megan Cummins never received her promised investment of $55,000 for 20 percent equity in her soap company. When she called to get the money, the shark reneged on the deal, asking for 50 percent equity for the same amount of money. With retailers asking for product, Cummins was put in a bad position. I had a similar situation in which an investor agreed in writing to fund my company, but pulled out at the last minute. I ended up in court to save the project. Also, in a recent Bloomberg television feature about TechStars, a business incubator, one company put its investment capital at great risk. One of the founders took money to pay personal financial obligations. The situation was later resolved, but may have been one of the reasons the team eventually split up.

3. *Business will immediately get better*. Again, not always true. In many cases, more money and resources translate into more problems. If the business plan and model are not sound, throwing more money at it will yield poor results. To illustrate, it can be like giving more money to a shopaholic. The ideal situation for having investors is when your company is experiencing certified, tremendous growth, a spurt that is outpacing your current resources. For example, Facebook nearly doubled its membership in 2004 to four hundred thousand. As a result, the company needed servers, so investor Sean Parker negotiated a deal in which Facebook's web host company, Western Technology Investment (WTI), gave the company a loan for $300,000. And some of WTI's executives invested their own funds in Facebook.

Understanding the downside to having investors in your business will better prepare you for the experience, if you choose to go that route. A capital infusion by an investor can be a huge accomplishment and really propel your business to the stratosphere of success, but remember that it can also be pure hell.

60) Focus on Building Revenue

My revenue was $4 million my first year in business, off of
one $20 item.
—Sara Blakely, billionaire, founder of Spanx

I attended an angel group meeting where my friend presented. His technology company, funded by the angel group, gave a brief update on the company's progress and took questions from the members of the angel group. A few years before this follow-up meeting, his company had received almost a $10 million investment by angels to spur rapid growth. Because of its unique business model and underlying patented technology, the company had tremendous promise, or at least that's what we thought until a candid question prompted an unsettling revelation.

During the five-minute presentation, my friend talked primarily about the impressive amount of earned media or free press that the company had received. It was featured in international and national media, ranging from print news to television. In fact, it was featured on a popular late-night television show that was a perfect fit for the target consumer it was attempting to reach.

The large amount of coverage the company received was great, but I thought it was a bit odd that the presentation was so focused on press coverage and not much else. I became very skeptical about the business's measurable progress. Apparently, the angels in the room shared my uneasiness. One of the angels addressed the concerns directly during the question and answer part of the presentation: "What are your revenues?"

There was an eerie silence in the room.

A normally poised and coherent CEO, my friend hesitated to answer the question. He was a bit stunned. His blank facial expression foreshadowed what happened next. After a poor introduction to his answer to mitigate the circumstances, he said sheepishly, "Around $5,000 a month." After his answer, I looked around the room at the faces of the angels, who are each high-net-worth indi-viduals and are veteran investors who have seen it all. They all looked unimpressed as my friend rambled on, trying to draw atten-tion away from the low numbers. Like I did, the angels sensed that the CEO was emphasizing the publicity his company received to cloak or to undermine the fact that his revenues were abysmal. I thought to myself that it was only a matter of time before his com-pany went under or was acquired.

Not even the millions of impressions received from a massive publicity campaign can hide the fact that you have poor sales. A company without sales is headed out of business or is really not even in business. In general, companies prove their viability through sales and indicate their level of success through profit. Technology companies are often an exception to this rule in the short term—as they may build value through increasing their user base, for example—but even these companies must show that they have true value by producing revenue.

Barbara Corcoran, a real-estate tycoon and angel investor known for her role on the television show *Shark Tank* said, "No sales equals no value to an investor." On her hit show, entrepre-neurs frequently have the same stunned face that my friend had when investors asked about revenue. Ironically, the entrepreneurs who have strong pitches proactively declare their revenue while those who have weak pitches timidly hide their revenue. I often find myself talking to the television when I watch *Shark Tank*, say-ing, "All of that is great, but what are your sales?" The sharks normally ask the same thing, which emphasizes that entrepreneurs should be focused on building revenue to increase their chances of an investment. Rarely do angels or venture capitalists invest in companies solely on the attractiveness of an idea.

The phrase attributed to champion boxer Joe Louis is quite ap-plicable to business when it comes to facing the inevitable matter of revenues: "You can run, but you can't hide." The revenue ques-tion always finds an entrepreneur, as my friend learned in an embarrassing way. He was running and trying to hide by emphasizing the wide acclaim that his company had received only to be gutted by the humbling revenue question. Investors didn't fall for his sleight of hand. They knew that publicity doesn't always translate into sales. It turns out that the angel investors were right on the money, literally. When I came up with the idea for writing this segment, I did a quick search on my friend's company. The tech company had just shut its doors and its supporting angel group cut its losses.

Entrepreneurs who ignore the revenue question only hurt themselves by overlooking the obvious. The best entrepreneurs ask the revenue question every day and focus on building value through sales. Everything else is less important.

61) The Biggest Investment in Your Company Is Yours

If I have nothing to sacrifice, I have nothing to gain.
—Catherine Ndereba, Kenyan marathon runner

Every now and then I attend angel investor meetings from which I draw much of my advice for young entrepreneurs. Being part of the early-stage, technology investment community affords me an exclusive opportunity to assess firsthand the quality of several start-ups.

In doing so, I see many of the mistakes that companies make when presenting their companies and ideas to angel investors. Criticism given behind closed doors or in personal conversations among angels is often more valuable than the feedback given after the official presentation to the body. Entrepreneur mistakes range from not preparing thoroughly to not answering a question asked by an angel during the dreaded question-and-answer period. Once in a blue moon, I come across a company that makes a mistake regarding its capital structure, giving angels a sound reason to doubt the commitment of the founders or top executives in the company.

Before speaking to the body of angels, the person presenting on behalf of the company seeking funds distributes the company's executive summary. This one- or two-page summary offers vital information in an easily readable tabular format—information like the business description, problem and solution, revenue model, board members, and funds sought. It also includes the company's current investment structure, which shows how much money the founders and other investors have put into the business.

In general, no matter how promising your business may be, investors want to know that you have some skin in the game. How much money you put into a business is a reflection of your own commitment to and belief in the business. Would you invest in a company whose founders have put little or no money into the company during its early stages? Probably not. You would at least like to know why the founder's investment is so small. Even if there is a technical founder on the team, for example, who has provided tens of thousands of dollars worth of sweat equity, it's always a good sign that he has also put hard cash into the business.

For example, one company presenting at a recent angel meeting I attended had two types of investors: The founders collectively invested $55,000, and they also had a $45,000 research grant. The company was requesting a six-figure investment. Another company with a more complex investment structure had six different investors, totaling just under $300,000 in investment capital. The founder alone had invested $200,000. His company was asking for a $500,000 investment to scale and to reach projected revenues of almost $8 million by 2015. These two companies are great examples of companies that put their money where their business is.

If you are seeking investment capital from an angel or a relative, be sure to quantify in clear terms the investment you've made in the company. Investors want to see that important information, which can increase your probability of getting funded. If you are

Iraising money in an unconventional way, you may have to quantify your input in an unconventional way. For instance, log the hours you've worked on your business and price your labor based on current market conditions. Or add up all the expenses you've had to pay to get the business to where it is. Do whatever it takes to validate your dedication to the business. A business whose founders are well-vested is a business that's worthier of investment.

62) Use Different Banks to Minimize Risk

I have always been afraid of banks.
—Andrew Jackson, seventh president, United States of America

One of the worst things you can do as an entrepreneur is to open a business bank account at a bank where you have a personal bank account. Likewise, it is not a good idea to open a business credit card at the same bank where you have a personal account. Should you ever have a financial problem with your business bank account or business credit card, your personal accounts will be affected negatively and vice versa.

Entrepreneurs often set up some or all of their banks accounts with the same bank for what they consider good reasons, but they do so without thinking of or knowing the consequences. For example, convenience is perhaps the most common reason. They prefer to go to the same bank, not several different banks, to make multiple transactions. Entrepreneurs are all about being efficient and saving time, but this benefit is nominal. Moreover, many entrepreneurs succumb to the banks' clever marketing and special offers that give privileges (like reward points or exempted fees) to customers who open multiple accounts. Entrepreneurs are all about saving money, but this, too, is not worth the small benefit.

So what's the problem? The problem is that banks don't treat multiple accounts they have linked to the same person separately. Regardless of what the accountholder may think or the impression

158

the banks may give, all of your accounts are linked together by your Social Security number and tax identification number. Unfortunately, the common misconception is that business accounts and personal accounts are somehow not connected and treated as separate liabilities. This is not always the case. While this may have been truer in the past, our sluggish economy has caused banks to change their methods of debt collection and to tighten their terms. Some banks are stricter than others.

An alarming but little-known problem is the fact that more business owners are experiencing a phenomenon known as *veil piercing*, a term used in corporate law that describes disregard for corporate entities. In other words, business owners who have set up a corporation to avoid personal liability are discovering that they can, in fact, be liable for certain debts. Banks and credit card companies are becoming more aggressive in pursuing debts. In fact, some are pushing the limits of their contractual abilities by overstepping legal boundaries to intimidate customers. Such coercive actions have spawned a deluge of complaints and lawsuits.

Also, to better manage risk and prevent losses, banks are more actively using the *right of offset*. Having multiple accounts with a bank makes it much easier for banks to go after debts and faster. For example, through right of offset, a bank can legally seize deposited funds to cover a loan that is in default. Imagine you missed a $750 loan payment for your business, and unexpectedly that exact amount is deducted from another bank account. That could spark many problems, costing you overdraft fees and one big headache. It happens frequently. What makes the matter trickier is that different states and different types of banks follow different right of offset laws.

In another disconcerting trend, business owners are beginning to see business credit card debts show up on their personal credit reports. Discover, for instance, has openly admitted to reporting business debts for placement on personal credit reports. Likewise, CapitalOne reports business debt of its credit card holders on personal credit reports. Most companies do not do this, but more are considering the policy. Also, know that if you have a personal credit card and business credit card with American Express, for example, it is monitoring your overall debt, not each account separately.

Unfortunately, many business owners have been denied personal credit because they were unaware that their business credit is now reported to personal credit bureaus. In one horror story, a business owner's business credit card company started to report to personal credit bureaus a few weeks before he planned to close on his new home. The company failed to communicate its new policy. As a result, his debt-to-income ratios worsened and his credit score tanked. He was denied a mortgage and was crushed.

In brief, always open your business bank account or business credit card with a bank that is not affiliated with the bank where you conduct important (especially personal) finances. By doing this, you minimize your risk of the bank doing something to jeopardize your financial welfare. Furthermore, read your terms for accounts and loans as if your life depended on it, and ask questions if you don't understand. You must have a strategy when opening bank accounts and applying for credit cards for your business, because they have a major effect on your financial future. If you don't take this crucial step, you are headed for disaster.

63) Know Your PAYDEX Score

A good reputation is more valuable than money.
—Publilius Syrus, Latin writer of maxims

While looking at the requirements of a Fortune 100 company's supply management division, I came across this statement: "Our selection process includes a review of D&B/Dun & Bradstreet (or comparable) reports." I was reminded of the many business owners I have come across who don't know what Dun & Bradstreet is and how this company can affect their business.

I take pride in having a high credit score or FICO score of 813 in the top 10 percent. Likewise, maintaining my business credit is just as important. In the business world, a company does not have a FICO score. Instead, it has a PAYDEX score, a rating maintained and calculated by Dun & Bradstreet. In other words, what the FICO score is to Equifax, the PAYDEX score is to Dun & Bradstreet.

According to its website, Dun & Bradstreet, or D&B for short, is the world's leading source of commercial information and insight on businesses. Its global commercial database contains more than 200 million business records, which provide customers with quality business information and the ability to make informed decisions. Customers primarily use D&B's resources to mitigate credit and supplier risk. D&B provides a wide range of business statistics such as liquidity ratios, asset management ratios, debt management ratios, and many other benchmarking tools. The most popular tool is the PAYDEX score.

The PAYDEX score is D&B's unique dollar-weighted numerical indicator of how a firm paid its bills over the past year, based on up to 55 percent trade experiences reported to D&B by various vendors. The D&B PAYDEX score ranges from 1 to 100, with higher scores indicating better payment performance. A score of 75 is roughly equivalent to a FICO score in the low 700s.

The D&B website is impressively thorough. You can view a sample of all three types of business credit reports with detailed explanations that D&B offers: the Basic Credit Report, the Standard Report, and the Premium Credit Report. The cost per report is $59.99, $119, and $159, respectively, as of summer 2012.

If you are in business and have requested credit before, chances are that a company has requested your D&B credit report. Many start-ups and small businesses are not even aware that they have a DUNS Number and corresponding credit report. Your creditors or vendors can report payment history about you, and D&B will assign you a D&B DUNS number. As with personal credit, be proactive in making sure that your company credit report is accurate and complete, that you find out your PAYDEX score, and that you learn how to obtain and to maintain the best report and PAYDEX score possible.

I strongly recommend that you read everything on the D&B website, because it is an essential step toward effectively managing your business credit, which helps to drive down costs and improve cash flow—not to mention it could be the determining factor that helps you close a big deal to become a supplier for a major company.

Chapter 5

Marketing & Sales

On any given Monday I am one sale closer and one idea away
from being a millionaire.
—Larry D. Turner, author, professional speaker

U ndoubtedly, marketing and sales are vital departments that reside at the heart of any business. In fact, many angel investors and venture capitalists agree that nothing is more important than being able to market and to sell your product or service. After all, a business with no sales is not much of a business at all.

This chapter presents useful tools to help develop your market and customer base. Likewise, you'll find advice for improving your ability to make a sale. Introduced with practical and engaging real-life cases, these suggestions can be implemented immediately and will give you results quickly.

---

64) You're in Sales, Whether You Want to Be or Not

Timid salesmen have skinny kids.
—Zig Ziglar, author, motivational speaker

Reality hit us like a Mack truck and stopped us dead in our tracks. Although we reached our goal of creating OmniPublisher, one of the first content management systems built specifically for newspapers and other periodicals, we realized that we forgot to include the most important element in our plan to make millions. Like so many other naïve but brilliant computer programmers, we focused on building the product, not selling it. When the first version of OmniPublisher was complete, we looked at each other and said, "Now what?" You'd expect more from a guy who would go on to write code for Goldman Sachs's trading division and a guy who was starting his third business, but you'll find that this is a common scenario among young entrepreneurs.

Entrepreneurs who start a business without thinking of how their products or services will be sold in the marketplace are making a huge mistake. Why?

First, *they run a high risk of wasting valuable resources to create a product or service that consumers do not want.* We are all familiar with huge flops. Some of my favorites and most egregious include Webvan, a 2001 dotcom, that delivered groceries to your home. The company reached almost $1 billion in total investment before it shut down. More recently, Netflix announced that it would be separating its online streaming service and its DVD mail service. Bad idea. Not only did customers reject this, but they also viciously attacked the company for implementing the change. The move cost Netflix 800,000 customers.

Second, *you are in business to make money.* That's the goal. As obvious as it sounds, some entrepreneurs forget this until it's too late. They realize it when they are too much in debt, when they have no operating income, or when they face some other coldwater-in-the-face moment. I remind myself every morning to focus on sales and profits. I think the title of George Cloutier's book put it best: *Profits Aren't Everything, They're the Only Thing*.

Companies that focus on sales and customer needs from the very beginning are more likely to be big winners. For instance, without Steve Jobs's talents in marketing and sales, Apple wouldn't have grown to be a public company with record sales. Steve Wozniak, who certainly was the technical brain behind the Apple I personal computer, wanted to give away his inventions. Jobs, on the other hand, was adamant about selling the Apple I and other products at a premium price. The rest is history. Similarly, Mark Zuckerberg had Eduardo Saverin, who began selling advertising for Facebook in April 2004. These ads included moving companies, T-shirt retailers, and other companies that sold college-related products and services.

Of course, there are rare exceptions. For example, Twitter was born out of a brainstorming session in 2006. The project didn't focus on sales and had no monetization strategy for years. Instead, the company honed in on developing the product and its user base. Also, Pandora took almost ten years to become profitable. These are great success stories, but most of us don't have the luxury or willingness to wait that long. We must be profitable as soon as possible.

The wise entrepreneur makes sales, the lifeline of any business, priority number one. An entrepreneur who has no interest in sales finds the best sales experts for the team to ensure the business's success. If you are like me, you sometimes focus too much on how great your product or service is. You assume that because it's the best thing since sliced bread, everyone will buy it. It rarely works that way, and finding out the hard way is too expensive.

By the way, if you were wondering, my business partner and I decided that *I* would market OmniPublisher to companies. Our decision was a huge mistake and stunted our growth. With the right sales talent and strategy, the value of the company would have been exponentially greater. I eventually sold the company, but for less than its full potential. It was a hard lesson to learn: If you build it, they do not necessarily come.

65) Your Customer Is Your Boss

The customer determines at the end of the day who is
successful and for what reason.
—Jerry Harvey, inventor, entrepreneur

Everyone talks about how entrepreneurship affords you freedom and independence to do what you want. No longer do you have to suffer the rigid and long hours of corporate America. Nor do you have a demanding and an insensitive boss breathing down your neck every minute. In many ways, these things are true. In fact, I am guilty of touting these benefits of entrepreneurship to spur interest in others to start a business. However, entrepreneurs gloss over reality by focusing on such half-truths.

What is reality? The reality is that even if you are an entrepreneur you have a boss: the customer. The idea that entrepreneurs are free of accountability is misguided and delusional. Ultimately, every business is accountable for meeting the needs of the customer. I learned this from the very first job I had as a computer programmer for IBM.

As a developer at IBM, I witnessed firsthand how some businesses can presumptuously ignore customer needs and dictate what users want. While working on a popular groupware product, I observed constant battles between product managers who dealt with customers and computer programmers who rarely, if ever, interacted with customers. On the one hand, product managers would translate feedback from users into product upgrades or changes to appease buyers. On the other hand, the developers would focus on creating challenging features that had no real benefits to the customers. The features may have been neat, but didn't add much value to the customers' businesses. In meeting after meeting, the same issues would arise and hot heads would clash. Often the developers would win, to the detriment of the ultimate users and IBM itself. The company needed to understand and focus on the reason the product and company existed. Neglecting the customer is a fatal mistake.

Although IBM, a blue-chip company, isn't representative of the average company, it does serve as a great example of how smaller companies and equally presumptuous entrepreneurs ignore their customers' input and feedback. Entrepreneurs, especially those who have experienced a degree of success, feel ordained to determine what is best for their customers, more than its customers are entitled to determine what is best for them. This attitude often manifests itself in the form of poor customer service or a slump in sales, often leading to a company going out of business.

Entrepreneurs in the business-to-business space must be especially careful to listen to their customers. As indicated in my IBM example, companies are less tolerant of features that don't add value to their organization. Perhaps this is why you see some major companies still using a non-Windows-based POS (Point of Sales) system. Their cash registers may look old to us, but they work and are cost-effective for them. As for companies in the business-to-consumer space, consumers are more forgiving and accepting of features that don't add value in a traditional business sense. For them, the value could be having the latest and greatest thing, or simply having a great experience with the product or service.

Major banks in the business-to-consumer space have recently had to deal with the backlash of customers who were unhappy with new fees for basic checking services. After a public relations nightmare, several banks finally budged and eliminated the monthly fee, Wells Fargo and Bank of America among them. By the time the banks reversed their new policy, thousands of customers had moved their accounts to credit unions. The major banks would lose more customers if they actually implemented the charges. Miffed customers and consumer activists created a Bank Transfer Day, a movement that garnered over fifty-eight thousand Facebook likes. The major retail banks learned the hard way that you must listen to your customers. Nowadays, with social media, you cannot act as if your customers do not exist. A few other companies that have notoriously ignored customer needs include Verizon Wireless for its new monthly data charge, BlackBerry for its geriatric products that haven't kept up with the times, and Circuit City for its terrible customer service.

Exceptions to this rule are few. Rarely can a company dictate to its customers what they need. Most exceptions come from technology companies like Apple, which have created and dominate new product categories. However, technology companies must be able to respond quickly to customer issues and suggestions, iterating as often as possible until they get the right formula. They may have more flexibility than other types of companies, but they, too, answer to the boss.

Just because you are an entrepreneur doesn't mean that you can't get fired. In fact, entrepreneurs get fired every day by dissatisfied customers. Ensure that you listen closely to your customers and respond to their changing needs in a quick fashion. If you introduce something new, be sure that you are prepared for the possibility that your suggestion could backfire.

66) You Have Sales before You Have a Business

Forget about the business outlook. Be on the outlook for business.
—Paul J. Meyer, author, businessman

I had no intention of becoming an entrepreneur. The thought never crossed my mind as a viable and sustainable option in life. In fact, I was conditioned to think and accept that getting and working a well-paying job was the Holy Grail, the consummate achievement in life. After finding a job, I then could get married, have kids, re-

169

tire, and die respectfully. Although I learned this restricted way of thinking at home, it was also reinforced in college. Every student worked hard to attain this *Pleasantville*-like life. Some days when all students were required to dress alike, I felt like an unoriginal product on an assembly line, being constructed for the corporate world. Not knowing anything else, I welcomed the process and final delivery to corporate America.

That all changed when a website I developed in college became very popular. It was so popular that I received inquiries from companies wanting to advertise. The first was from a dotcom called JobDirect, a web-based job-matching service for college students. JobDirect's inquiry caught me completely off-guard, because I had no intention of selling ads on my website. I built the site for fun and to hone my web development skills. I simply wanted it to be the best college portal on the Web, and some would say that it was. In other words, I was passionate about the product, not profits.

JobDirect was eager to advertise on my website and to have everything prepared for the back-to-school period, so negotiations about price and ad placement went quickly. I was clueless about the whole process, so I searched online for any information to help me appear like I knew what I was doing. I had no idea what to charge the company, how to structure the deal, or who the decision-maker was. I gave JobDirect's VP of campus relations an arbitrary figure for the cost of the banner ad that made hardly any sense. Surprisingly, he accepted it without hesitation. I probably could have charged more. By summer of my junior year, I had closed a partnership and deal with JobDirect that earned me an $1,800 check. When I received the check via FedEx, I copied it and framed it. I was especially proud. My handsel wouldn't be the normal wrinkled dollar bill you often see hanging on a business's wall, but a big check. However, there was just one problem: I couldn't cash the check.

My website was not officially set up as a business, so I had a rather large check made out in my website's name and no way to cash it. However, with that much money at stake, I learned fast what I had to do in order to open a bank account. I researched online the necessary steps to become an official business and followed each one. In fact, I used an online legal service to organize my articles of incorporation and file for my business license. Similarly, I submitted online my application for an Employee Identification Number (EIN) with the IRS. Lastly, I took my articles of incorporation, business license, EIN, and two forms of identification to the local Wachovia and opened my business account. I was in business.

I didn't know it at the time, but having sales before having a business was proof that I had a promising venture. In fact, considering all the businesses I have started—and there have been many—the most successful ones were those that had sales or significant demand before I even incorporated. There is no better way to start a business than with purchase orders. I had no idea what I was doing, but it was the best situation possible.

As a result, I am weary of those who go into business for the sake of being in business. On the other hand, I get excited about those who have a dynamic product or service that serves a salivating market. Which one are you?

67) You Aren't Always the Best Person to Close a Deal

> Beauty awakens the soul to act.
> —Dante Alighieri, Italian poet

Excited to hit the pavement and to sell advertisements for my new magazine, I visited a local mom-and-pop store near my alma mater, Morehouse College. After my sales pitch, I waited to hear if the business owner would place an ad in my next issue. He didn't buy an ad, but he did give me something much more valuable than an order: unfiltered advice on how to make him a customer. The owner, who was in his mid-forties and brutally honest, said, "Kevin, I love your magazine, and I think placing an ad in it would really help my business, but I will never buy from *you*. Send your editor here, and I'll buy an ad from her every month!"

Chelsey, the editor of my magazine at the time, was one of the main reasons the magazine was so popular, and it wasn't necessarily because she was a great editor. Every month, college-aged men with raging hormones would rush to pick up the latest issue of the magazine to see Chelsey's beautiful picture on her editor's page. Likewise, she had a large fan club of older men who were just as eager to see her picture. When the business owner asked me to send Chelsey to visit him, I just smiled because I knew that was the only thing I could do to convince him to buy an ad. I obliged.

Before this eye-opening experience, I thought my customers would buy ads primarily for logical reasons like great prices, a large circulation, or quality content. Never did I think that customers would buy ads for other, seemingly frivolous reasons. I was wrong and learned quickly to better understand and to assess a potential customer's psyche, which gives clues on how to close that person. In doing so, I had to come to the realization that in many cases, I, the CEO of the company, was not always the best person to close a deal. As in the case of this local business owner, sometimes people would much rather buy from a future Miss USA contestant (Chelsey) than an enterprising geek (me), no matter how logically sound the geek's offer is.

Nowadays, I see myself as the leader of a team of superstars who can close just about anyone. Like the owner of a winning professional sports team, I have put together a group of outstanding people who can handle many different types of situations come game time. To increase the likelihood of a sale, we research our prospects and determine the best plan of action. For example, if a potential customer shows signs that she will respond better to a male, we send a male. In the same way that the Los Angeles Lakers coaching staff watches hours of film to determine player matchups, we find out as much as we can about our prospects to decide who should go on the sales call. Our approach is tremendously effective and renders great results through increased profits.

Despite the proven results of this strategy, many entrepreneurs have a serious problem with it. They think like I thought. They mistakenly believe that we have a utopian free market in which buyers operate on logic alone. In other words, buyers don't judge offers by the person making the offer; they can see past their own assumptions, stereotypes, impressions, and desires. Unfortunately, we are far from this point.

In a recent CNN feature *Black in America: The New Promised Land, Silicon Valley*, a multimillionaire entrepreneur of Indian descent ruffled some feathers with his candid advice. He encouraged young African American entrepreneurs to "get a white guy to be your front man." The implications of his advice are certainly disappointing and sad, but I agree with him wholeheartedly. Ultimately, it's about giving the merit of your offer the best chance possible. The entrepreneur's job is not to reform the buyer. Instead, understand what makes the customer tick and adjust.

The best entrepreneurs know that being a CEO doesn't make you the best person to present to investors, to close a sale, or to do a number of other tasks. Perhaps you don't speak with passion or you have trouble communicating. In this case, you must be willing and able to adjust to different situations to maximize your opportunities. As it relates to understanding your talents and gifts, Morehouse College alumnus Dr. Martin Luther King Jr. put it best in one of his sermons: "A Ford car trying to be a Cadillac is absurd, but if a Ford will accept itself as a Ford, it can do many things that a Cadillac could never do: it can get in parking spaces that a Cadillac can never get in." King finalizes his thought, saying, "The principle of self-acceptance is a basic principle in life." I concur, and entrepreneurs who understand this principle in business are exponentially more successful.

68) Networking Isn't All about You

The currency of real networking is not greed but generosity.
—Keith Ferrazzi, founder, CEO, Ferrazzi Greenlight

I hate networking. Well, I should qualify my statement. I hate what networking has become in many instances. As a result, I have altogether stopped going to self-proclaimed "exclusive networking events," because they yield such poor results and waste my precious time.

Instead of quality experiences that facilitate exchanges and lead to business relationships, many networking events are nothing more than a mini-convention of extremely self-centered people. You know these narcissistic types. Often they are the professional networkers who are dressed to draw too much attention, reek of disingenuousness, and heap their business cards on you before you can say hello. When they speak to you, the subtext of everything they say is, "I am the greatest! This is why you should buy my product or service. Now, off to the next person." If I find myself in a conversation with such an individual, I watch the mouth move, but all I hear is, "Me, me, me." Some may fool you for a second by asking about your company, but then it's back to, "I, I, I." If you have the courage after ten, fifteen, or twenty minutes of their shameless monologues—time you'll never get back—you just leave them. They may not even notice you've left.

When done correctly and effectively, networking isn't about you. Rather, it's about what you can do to help others improve their businesses. Imagine if business owners asked you the following questions at a networking event instead of talking aimlessly about themselves: "What is the best type of customer for your business?" "If I come across someone in my network, how would I know that this person is a good customer for you?" "What specifically can I do to help your business grow?" What a difference! The likelihood of you doing business directly with someone you just met is small. However, the likelihood of you being able to help this person to find customers within your network is much greater. This attitude of service rather than self-service has made a huge difference in my business. In fact, I use this approach all the time. It works during networking events and other situations.

Two great benefits come with this paradigm shift. First, the discussion gets right to how a relationship can help both of you grow. Little time is wasted on pretense. Most people will be shocked by your focus and unselfish willingness to help with exactly what they need, and they will naturally catch on and return the favor. If not, you can always tell them how they can help you. Second, this approach builds rapport faster than any other method. People are more inclined to trust those who are willing to help and eventually do.

Most people starting a business are especially excited about networking. The idea seems like the smart thing to do in order to grow a business. However, after a while, many discover that the main result is a stack of useless business cards. Some people end up like me, disillusioned by networking.

I am being a bit extreme, though. I am not encouraging you to avoid networking events entirely, but if you choose to attend them, get the most out of your experience by assuming an attitude of service. Ultimately, it will come back to you multiple times.

69) Don't Waste Time on People Who Can't Say Yes

Never allow a person to tell you no who doesn't have
the power to say yes.
—Eleanor Roosevelt, former First Lady, United States of America

Few things are more irritating in business than dealing with a person who pretends to be a decision-maker but in reality is just a subordinate. You know these misleading types. They may indeed work for a company that you hope to establish as a client, and they may even have a title implying influence, but they are in no way able to authorize anything. In the rare case that they are able to suggest a deal, the request must go through so much approval and red tape that developing a strong relationship with this individual was, in hindsight, probably not worth the effort. It would have been easier to find the real decision-maker. Businesspeople waste billions of work hours calling, dining, and persuading these tricksters in hopes of garnering some business only to find out that their efforts were in vain. They eventually learn the hard way that if they can't buy, you won't sell.

This problem has no easy solution, but I have found one way to manage the situation quite effective. As you work your way through the different layers of people in search of a decision-maker, simply be direct. Specifically, ask your contact once you've shared your intentions, "Who will make the final decision on this?" You could also phrase it this way: "Who are the other people who will be included in making a final decision on this?" In most cases, your contact will answer your question with the same directness you used. Asking questions like these significantly cuts down on the time you spend trying to sell someone who cannot buy.

These questions are open-ended, meaning they cannot be answered with a simple yes or no. If you pose these questions in a yes-or-no format, they lose their potency. Asking an open-ended question in this situation forces the person answering to provide vital information that empowers you to be most effective. These types of questions leave little room for interpretation or misunderstanding. In fact, you should use open-ended questions in business as often as you can.

This tactic does not give you a license to neglect or mistreat people who are between you and the ultimate decision-maker. Tread lightly and treat everyone involved in the process with the utmost respect, from the secretary to the CEO. You want those who aren't necessarily decision-makers but influencers to also buy in to what you propose. Insiders, those who work for the company you hope to bring on as a client, have influence on decision-makers. Sometimes these individuals yield more influence than you think. Your goal should be to draft them onto your team so that they can sell your idea from the inside.

This small but powerful change had an immediate impact on my business when I adopted it, from faster results when selling to more interested investors when pitching. After asking the suggested questions, I received clarity; I knew exactly whom my target was. Without such vital information you are throwing darts while blindfolded, wishing to hit the bull's-eye. That's no way to run a successful business. Take off the blindfold by using this approach and increase your chances for getting a yes.

70) There's No Such Thing as a Cold Call

A winning effort begins with preparation.
—Joe Gibbs, former NFL coach, race team owner

At a recent entrepreneurship conference where there was a panel with angel investors, an audience member asked the following questions, "Do you take cold calls? And if you do, what should I, as a business owner seeking capital, say?" One of the panelists, Valerie Gaydos, founder and president of Capital Growth, answered the question like most people would expect an angel investor to. She responded that she doesn't take cold calls. Instead, she screens potential companies with her partners who bring her quality companies. However, Timothy Reese, managing partner and general manager of Forge Intellectual Capital, surprised everyone by saying, "I *do* take cold calls, but your call shouldn't be cold." Everyone in the audience perked up to hear his advice on how to effectively reach out to an angel investor who knows nothing about you or your company.

When giving his candid advice, Reese emphasized that you

must first know as much about his company as possible. For instance, if you are looking for an investment in your apparel company and his firm doesn't invest in those types of companies, you are wasting your time. It is imperative that you research the types of deals that an angel has done and prefers so that you have a better chance of catching the angel's attention. Furthermore, you should know the size of the deals, and if the information is available, how those deals were structured. It requires quite a bit of research and hard work on your end, but as another angel, Daymond John, on the panel mentioned, this could be the big deal of your life. You don't want to go in totally cold and "botch" the opportunity.

If you are an elite entrepreneur, you don't go into anything cold. Whether you are selling a product or selling your company to an investor, you should know as much as you can about the prospect. Nowadays, there is no excuse for being unprepared. A plethora of informational resources are at hand, the Internet being the most common. Entrepreneurs who go the extra mile to better position themselves in a sale always come out better than an entrepreneur who tries to wing it.

The biggest benefit of doing your homework is instantly establishing trust and credibility with your prospect, which goes a long way. As angel investor Reese suggested in his advice, an entrepreneur who approaches him and knows his background instantly earns his respect and ear. Likewise, your cold calls can warm up quickly when you've researched your prospects thoroughly. They will appreciate your efforts to understand their position.

Here's one technique that exhibits how you can establish rapport when making cold calls. Don't focus only on yourself or your product when you communicate with a prospect for the first time. Instead, mention the vital information that your research revealed. For illustration purposes, let's say that your investigation uncovered the prospect's previous buying history and their need to cut costs. You could start a conversation by saying, "I understand that you have purchased from company A in the past, but I would love to share with you how our product has been rated the highest quality by an independent source and costs less." By saying this, you've done two important things: earned trust by reviewing the prospect's buying history and sparked interest with a way to reduce costs. Using techniques like this gives you a great advantage over your competition.

The likelihood of closing a sale is directly linked to the preparation that goes into making that sale. Before you attempt to persuade any prospect your way, take the time to find out as much as you can about the person. You'll never have a cold call again.

71) Tell Everyone about Your Business

Kids: they dance before they learn there is anything that isn't music.
—William Stafford, poet

For the past two years, I have had the privilege of being an instructor for the Teenpreneur conference, a two-day program that has taught thousands of teens the vital concepts of entrepreneurship. Along with other instructors who are entrepreneurs, I have instructed young students on how to write a business plan, how to sell, how to select a business concept that they love, and where they can find help to build their business. The program also brings some of the most successful entrepreneurs and business executives to talk to the teens. For example, the CEO of Capri Investment Capital (Quintin E. Primo III), who manages assets of over $3.6 billion, came to the conference in 2012 and talked about how he has built his trailblazing company. I enjoy teaching and working with the teens because they are focused and excited to learn how to build wealth through entrepreneurship. I really love the fact that many students already have thriving businesses, even as teenagers.

Every year we have a handful of students who already have businesses that make money. This year, a young lady who makes customized balloon shapes and animals attended our sessions. She started her company at the age of nine after she received a kit that showed her how to make balloon art. Now, as elegant and well-spoken as any adult CEO, the sixteen-year-old manages a thriving business with corporate clients. With 2011 revenues topping $5,500, she is expanding her business to include other party services like face painting and storytelling. Another teenager, fifteen-years-old, bakes delicious cookies. As stated in her company's professional brochure, she is "baking her way into college." A couple of young men who are juniors in high school have an artist management company. They break new artists based on a successful formula that they have developed. In fact, the two men won the conference's pitch competition, which required them to woo a panel of three judges by describing their business in three minutes. Moreover, a fourteen-year-old young woman had started a concession stand at her church to serve mainly people who have no time to eat breakfast before church. She has made good money with her clever business.

In addition to these teenagers being truly inspiring, they taught us adults a basic lesson that many older and veteran entrepreneurs struggle with. The lesson? Entrepreneurs should tell everyone about their business and do it unapologetically.

With no fear, each of the students who had a business talked to everyone at the conference about their business. For example, the young lady with the balloon creation and entertainment company arrived at the conference thirty minutes before it began with sample balloons in hand. She was dressed in a business suit and eager to tell every person who came to the conference her business's story. The youngster with the concession stand business brought her basket of candy and was selling it to everyone, including parents who came the final day for the graduation ceremony. She was working hard. I was especially impressed with her initiative. For instance, she bought a large bag of candy from a conference participant who won it for volunteering. The participant didn't want the bag of candy, so she bought it from him for much less than its worth and sold each packaged unit for a quarter. She later told me (after I bought some candy) that she made twice as much as she paid for it; she was even making deals during the conference. Other teens were making sales and spreading the word about their babysitting service, lawn care service, bakery, and so on. They had no fear, and if they did, you certainly couldn't tell.

Toward the end of the conference, one of my co-instructors pointed out that for whatever reason, many adults lose or never develop their fearless ability to tell others about their business. Strangely, some entrepreneurs think that they will magically receive business for being passive and not bothering others. They confuse being humble with being quiet. Another possible reason for their reticence is conditioning. The same instructor mentioned, "I am from the South, and women aren't encouraged to be forward. We aren't taught to be aggressive and to tell people about our businesses." Moreover, some entrepreneurs are simply afraid of a negative response. Whatever the reason, a lot of business is lost because inhibited entrepreneurs have decided that telling others about their business is offensive, pompous, inconvenient, or counterproductive.

An entrepreneur who doesn't tell people about his or her business is like a baseball player at bat who swings only when it's sunny, missing a lot of good pitches that could be home runs. The passive entrepreneur serves no one except the competition by staying quiet. We all know that business doesn't come easy and that you may not naturally be a people person, but you have to get out of your comfort zone. The rules of the game are to take advantage of every opportunity you have, which means engaging other people. Otherwise, you will never maximize your potential. Like a fearless teenage entrepreneur, develop the habit of telling everyone about your business. It will make a significant difference. Besides, if you don't, I know some sharp teenagers who are willing and able to take the business if you are too scared to pursue it.

72) Ask the Right Questions

Successful people ask better questions, and as a result, they get better answers.
—Tony Robbins, author, professional speaker

As an entrepreneur, your success depends greatly on your ability to ask the right questions. However, few people understand the enormous value of mastering this art. I would argue that several entrepreneurs—business professionals, too—have no idea that the quality of the questions they ask determines their fate.

Why is mastering the art of asking good questions not a high priority on the list of skills to acquire for entrepreneurs? Perhaps we assume that all questions are created equal, and that's simply not true. Depending on the situation, there are good questions and bad questions. Being able to determine the difference gives you a competitive advantage in business. Let's examine exactly what good and bad questions are.

In general, a bad question is one that doesn't encourage a substantive answer. For example, if you have just received an order from a new customer, "Shall I send you an invoice?" is a poor question. This question can be answered quite easily without any detailed information that could help you speed up the entire payment process, not to mention that the answer is quite obvious. The prospect may simply answer, "Yes." Of course, you could follow up with another question—"How long will it take for payment?"— but you now sound a bit imposing and impatient. A good question in this situation would be, "What are the steps you have to go through to issue payment?" This question invokes a much more thorough answer without an imposing follow-up question. Perhaps the client reveals in the answer that one of the steps is issuing a check from a third party, which takes at least a week. Knowing this, you can now offer suggestions to expedite the payment process, such as encouraging the client to pay with a credit card because you offer a 5 percent discount.

Asking the right questions after an objection is perhaps the most important time when this skill comes in handy. Customers rarely share the true reasons behind their hesitations, and the right questions can reveal those reasons. For instance, to overcome an objection about price, try asking, "What kind of return on investment are you expecting?" After cleverly exposing the truth through good questions, you can directly address objections, improving your chances of winning over an individual. Likewise, addressing objections in this way helps entrepreneurs with vetting or refining a start-up idea.

A common impediment that customers have is high cost. In several negotiations, customers have complained that my price is too high. After asking them, for example, to describe their budgetary process, I might learn that cost is often not the issue. Frequently, customers overspend their budgets for a given time period, in which case you could invoice them during two separate periods or suggest that they share the costs with another department with available funds. You can receive the full value for your product or service if you know the right questions to ask. A bad question or simply not asking any question after an objection could cost you that million-dollar deal.

Avoid closed-ended questions, which can be answered with a simple yes or no. In general, open-ended questions are much better than simple yes-or-no questions. For instance, instead of asking a potential customer if she is satisfied with a competitor's product or service, ask specifically what she likes and dislikes about it. This information is highly valuable and helps you position your company to win her business.

In his book *Questions That Sell*, author Paul Cherry writes, "Research has shown that during typical business interactions customers reveal only 20 percent of what is on their minds. . . . It is your responsibility to get to the other 80 percent." The best entrepreneurs get to this other 80 percent by asking the right questions and turning the answers into an irresistible business solution. As you continue to improve your skills, whether in selling or product development, focus on mastering the art of asking great questions to take your business to the next level. There's no question (pun intended) that you'll see an improvement immediately.

73) Receive the Maximum Value for Your Products or Services

Our belief was that if we kept putting great products in front of customers, they would continue to open their wallets.
—Steve Jobs, cofounder, Apple

As a sophomore in college, I cofounded a Latin jazz band called Río Negro with a Puerto Rican friend of mine who played congas. We loved everything about Latin music and soon found other musicians from our school to join the band. After becoming popular on campus, we began to do more high-profile performances around Atlanta, even playing for Super Bowl XXXIV and President Bill Clinton. During those early days, we played most performances for free while we established our name and honed our style. However, as our popularity grew, we began to accept paying gigs from corporations and organizations willing to pay us. We had no idea what to charge or how to charge. As the bandleader I determined our rates and handled the band's business.

For a long time, we thought that the amount we charged for our performances was standard. The problem was that our standard was pretty low, contrary to the high quality of music we produced. We didn't learn about how low our standard was until a veteran musician in town called our attention to it. This veteran jazz guitarist had a reputation for being brutally blunt. In fact, he was infamous for kicking subpar musicians off stage at jam sessions. In that characteristic cool and nonchalant tone that all old jazz musicians have, he complained, "You young cats are doin' big gigs for a few hundred dollars. These are $2,000 gigs, man. You are messin' with my money!" One of my band members actually got into a spat with the disgruntled man during a commercial break for a radio station interview. They just happened to be there at the same time.

Realizing that our standard was indeed too low and considering that we wanted to make a living from music, I decided to increase our rates significantly. I thought that the change would be as simple as raising the rates and collecting bigger checks. I was wrong: It didn't quite work out that way. Several of our prospects had sticker shock, hearing the higher rates and almost always saying no thanks. As a result, I reverted to our lower rates, thinking that this was the only way we would get gigs. Before long, we resented the grind for such little pay. It just wasn't as fun anymore. I decided to try something new: sticking firmly to the higher rates and not giving in.

For months, we didn't get many gigs, but I stuck to the plan with my band members' support. I received several rejections, but I would also hear and sense genuine disappointment from those who wanted to hire us but couldn't. People really wanted our band to play for their events. Some even told me that they would request a larger budget the next year so that they could hire us. Sure enough, the next year several of the companies and organizations that couldn't afford us before found the money to secure us at the rate we requested. Apparently, telling these clients no built our value tremendously. It was as if they respected us for holding our ground. The strategy seemed counterintuitive at first, but it worked. Our brand and reputation grew as we demanded and received higher pay.

From this experience, I learned a valuable lesson that I apply in my other businesses: Set your price or rate and demand that you get it. This requires you to respectfully say no when prospects ask you to lower your rate, but in many cases they will respect you more for holding your ground and may come back later willing to pay. You'll also need extra patience, because it will take time to develop the demand for your company, especially if you have to wait for a new annual budget. Sometimes I unabashedly suggest that my potential buyer request more money from their company to meet our prices.

Of course, this strategy requires that you offer the best quality available. You can't demand top dollar if your product or service can be easily substituted. My band was unique in the Atlanta market, giving us a significant competitive advantage and demand. We played a type of music that not many bands played in our city, and we did it well. No one pays a premium price for poor quality—at least not twice.

Novice entrepreneurs often make the mistake of devaluing the worth of their product or service. While lowering your price may be an effective way to enter a market or to gain customers, it eventually corrodes profitability in the long term. Companies that compete on price alone tend to go out of business quickly. Strive to stay in business for decades like Apple. The most valuable company in the world in August 2012 with a market capitalization of $619 billion, Apple has never compromised on demanding high prices for its products. At the same time, it has never compromised on delivering excellent products. As with Apple and several other premium brands, high quality and high prices can make your company a winner, too. Now that should be music to your ears.

74) Don't Patronize Customers

Companies don't get rich hurting their customers.
—John Stossel, consumer reporter

At a private business club I introduced a friend of mine to an important prospective client who could bring him a lot of business. While introducing him, I emphasized his recent accomplishment of being featured in an issue of a national business magazine. Because of my warm introduction and endorsement, the prospect was especially excited about my friend's business and how it could help her. I was sure that he had already won her business. Naturally, my friend asked for her contact information to follow up, but after taking it, he ruined his chances of closing the deal.

After he took her e-mail address and phone number, he said with a flat, uninterested tone, "I'll have my assistant give you a call tomorrow." I wanted to grab him by the shoulders, shake him a few times, and scold him for doing what he just did. I didn't need to, though. His prospect retorted, "I want *you* to call me!" It was too late. In less than five seconds, he managed to jeopardize tens of thousands of dollars in new business and to tarnish what started off as a great first impression for his service-oriented company.

I often witness young entrepreneurs make this cardinal mistake: patronizing customers to appear professional. In doing so, they alienate their customers and cut off their own limbs. You know it as soon as it happens. Perhaps the most egregious example is when a founding CEO pushes you off to an assistant, like my friend did. The examples are virtually endless of the pompous CEO who does more harm than good.

Why do entrepreneurs and CEOs act this way? In many instances, they don't know that they are wrong or that their actions are harmful. Other times, the action is quite deliberate. Young CEOs—and they're not alone—patronize their customers for four main reasons.

1. *They think that CEOs are supposed to act this way.* They have an ill-conceived notion of what a CEO is and how a CEO acts. Nowhere does it say in the definition of CEO that you must act as if you are not accessible or that you are above customers and the people who work for you.

2. *They take a bit too far the common advice to delegate.* CEOs indeed must be good at delegating. This skill reinforces clear roles within the company and helps to manage time. However, you must

use common sense, too. It's not as easy as methodically directing certain tasks to certain people regardless of the context. Especially when dealing with customers directly, delegating requires a certain level of finesse. For instance, my friend at least should have asked the prospect if it was alright to have his assistant call her. Ideally, if he were actually that busy or had strict policies on protocol, he would have called her the next day to establish trust and to explain his company's order process from that point on.

3. *Their ego is too big for their own good.* Just because you have a business and you are an entrepreneur doesn't give you license to be condescending to anyone. In fact, it has nothing to do with business. In general, people dislike arrogant people. Arrogant CEOs, especially leaders of start-ups, need a consistent dose of humility. Ironically, most of them are just a few irate clients away from failure.

4. *They want to give the impression that they lead a big business.* Somehow young CEOs delude themselves into believing that clients respect bigger companies more or that their highly professional front can justify higher prices. To the contrary, my experience has been that this is not a favorable assumption for most entrepreneurs. No matter how large your company may be, if your brand is unfamiliar, you won't necessarily benefit from the extra respect that a Fortune 500 company receives. Respect mostly comes from how you treat customers individually and the high quality of your work. You aren't fooling anyone but yourself.

Like my friend, you may need an *Undercover Boss* reality check. Even if you are the CEO of your company, never make clients feel less than they are. There is no justification for it at all. Your job is to make your clients and your employees feel as if they are the most important people in the world.

75) Build Your Network Creatively

It isn't just what you know, and it isn't just who you know. It's actually who you know, who knows you, and what you do for a living.
— Bob Burg, best-selling author, *Endless Referrals*

If you go to hit-or-miss networking events to build your business, you probably aren't making the best of your time. The value of networking in the traditional sense where random people meet and try to connect the dots is next to nil. In fact, the value may be negative and is therefore hurting your business.

For a moment years ago, many people thought that this kind of networking was getting an upgrade. In 2001, entrepreneurs and professionals from all fields welcomed the new idea of NetWeaving, a concept introduced by author and businessman Bob Littell. NetWeaving, as described by the book that teaches the technique, is "all about giving and helping others while having the confidence to know that eventually you, the NetWeaver, will benefit in return." This strategy is more effective than traditional networking, but it still doesn't give you a direct plan of attack. Moreover, you could possibly find business for everyone else, and the favors never return to you, or they just take too long to do so. Consequently, the NetWeaving craze didn't last long at all.

Networking should take on a different meaning to you as an entrepreneur. It should not only mean going to an event in hopes that you'll meet someone there who can help you grow your business. Instead, it should mean following these four important steps:
1. Being proactive
2. Being creative
3. Meeting the right people (what I often call "check writers")
4. Finding the most appropriate environment

Networking this way gives you the best chance at actually closing a major deal, and that's what it is all about.

For example, I have found that volunteering for charities and nonprofits provides a great opportunity for me to meet C-level and director-level professionals who can authorize a deal with my company. First, this strategy meets the proactive requirement. Volunteerism is not for wimps. It demands a commitment to and accountability from others. Second, it meets the creative test. Most people wouldn't put volunteerism and networking together. Third, it gets me to the right people. Many corporate decision-makers are proud of the charities they support. In fact, some companies strongly encourage that their employees give a portion of their time to charities like Habitat for Humanity. Naturally, leaders take part in these initiatives to encourage the involvement of the rest of their team. Fourth, I'm in a "no selling" environment that instantly builds rapport. When a prospect sees you volunteering for a charity, the shared experience reflects well on you. Also, it evokes a good feeling in a prospect that increases the likelihood of doing business.

Years ago I saw a huge growth opportunity in doing business with financial institutions. I identified a nonprofit that was well-sponsored by the companies I wanted to have as clients, including Wells Fargo, Nationwide, Bank of America, and H&R Block. I also was able to find the individuals in these large companies who volunteered at the nonprofit and learn their corporate roles. Next, I offered my time and resources to the nonprofit, which teaches financial literacy and entrepreneurship to high school and college students. To make a long story short, I met many C-level supporters who wrote or authorized checks for the nonprofit. Moreover, the CEO of the nonprofit, seeing my dedication to his organization, gave me excellent introductions to his check-writing sponsors. As a result, my company ended up doing a lot of business with these companies and continues to do so today.

I cannot guarantee you that following this specific example will work for your business, but I can say that following the four rules outlined will help you become more effective in getting to the right people. As opposed to hoping to meet the right people at an event, guarantee your presence with decision-makers by implementing this methodology. You won't win using old networking techniques.

76) Don't Hold Grudges

Anger dwells only in the bosom of fools.
—Albert Einstein, German physicist

Entrepreneurship is a humbling exercise in learning how to deal with your negative feelings, so as to do what's best for your company. One of the most difficult feelings to tame is anger caused by a prospective customer who finds no value in your product or service and tells you so. I come across this situation often when mentoring young entrepreneurs who are so confident about their company that they really believe their offer is the best thing since sliced bread. They think, *How can anyone say no to what we have to offer?* In what they think is a retaliatory move, they curse the prospective customer. They convert a no that they received into a "never" by writing off the prospect.

I can certainly relate to this feeling of anger and disappointment that stems from rejection. It was especially intense when I courted customers, especially big ones, that for no apparent reason suddenly reneged on their commitment to buy. I vividly remember pursuing a Fortune 100 client for years. Finally, it agreed to sign a multiyear, six-figure contract, only to disappear when the time came to sign on the dotted line. I couldn't believe that the deal fell through in that way. A novice entrepreneur, I was bitter and vowed never to have anything more to do with the company.

The phrase "This is business, not personal" made popular in *The Godfather* certainly applies to this lesson. You must not take business "personal" because it pushes you off track and leads to terrible business decisions. Instead, transform rejection or a negative occurrence in your business to positive energy that helps you persevere. That's the mark of a veteran entrepreneur.

The simplest rule to follow in any business relationship is to treat even those who reject you like they are your biggest and best clients. Be courteous at all times, send thank-you notes, and provide them with information to help them in their business. These are just a few suggestions on how to maintain a positive reputation and boost chances of any opportunity in the future. Don't write them off by speaking ill of them, suspending future contact, removing them from your mailing list, or even wishing them harm. Whatever you do, don't cease communication, because conditions could change for the better at any moment; when they do, you'll want the client to feel that the lines of communication have always been open.

As an entrepreneur, your ability to turn anger caused by rejection into motivation to persevere can take your company to soaring heights. Negative feelings can be your worst enemy, causing you to miss huge opportunities. I almost missed a big one. The Fortune 100 company I mentioned earlier that pulled out of a major deal did come around much later. My change in fortune may have come from killing them with kindness. It doesn't pay to hold grudges in business. If you do, you can only be angry with yourself.

Chapter 6

Leadership

Leadership and learning are indispensable to each other.
—John F. Kennedy, thirty-fifth president, United States of America

L eaders are born, not made. What do you think? Many people disagree. While some people seem to come out of the womb with leadership qualities, they don't have a monopoly on leadership, especially when it comes to business.

Leadership qualities can be taught and learned. Countless examples are available of tech entrepreneurs who learned to be leaders of their companies—and are quite good ones. Mark Zuckerberg, the cofounder of Facebook who was coached by business veterans, comes to mind. Once a reserved geek, he is now a dynamic CEO of a billion-dollar company.

In this chapter, you read about some of the main leadership qualities that entrepreneurs have and why they are important.

77) Act in Spite of How You Feel

A clear understanding of negative emotions dismisses them.
—Vernon Howard, author, philosopher

If I had missed this huge opportunity, my company would have possibly left millions on the table.

During the previous two nights, I had gotten three hours of sleep. I was exhausted and needed rest badly. My eyes were blood-shot, I had a slight headache, and I was growing irritable. During a national conference for entrepreneurs, I was working diligently as an instructor, finishing up a major project for my company, working on a new book, and entertaining friends who were also in town. I was overwhelmed. I was used to a less intensive schedule. To make matters more challenging, I was still adjusting to a time-zone change.

During the last night of the conference, when attendees were dressed in their best suits and gowns to enjoy the culminating gala and enthusiastic to make final contacts, my mind was elsewhere. While I should have been energetic and ready to speak with every-one I could about my business, I was more concerned with eating dinner and going to sleep afterward. I couldn't wait for the end of the conference so I could rest.

As I walked around the ballroom noticing the different tables labeled with Fortune 100 sponsors, I passed the table of a large financial services company that for months I had been trying to gain as a client. When I saw the table, I was instantly reminded that one of the main reasons I attended the conference was to pursue new business for my new start-up, a data analytics company. As opposed to many of the other corporate tables, the financial services company table was full of representatives from the company. At this moment I was determined to not let my sleep deprivation ruin my chances of making a great connection.

Realizing the need to take advantage of the big opportunity, I eventually overcame my lethargy and unwillingness to connect with people. I conjured up every ounce of energy left in my body. With newfound strength and excitement, I gave the entire table my sixty-second pitch. At first I thought it didn't go over well. By the looks on their faces, they seemed uninterested. I thought that my words had fallen on deaf ears, but then things turned for the good. One gentleman next to where I was standing at the table turned toward me and said that he was interested in my product. He understood the concept instantly and genuinely seemed excited about it. Before I knew it, he handed me his business card and told me to contact him.

This gentleman was a company vice president in charge of buying the technology that my company offers. What I had tried to do for months just occurred in a few seconds, all because I was able to push through the inertia of my negative feelings. If I had let my emotions rule, I would have walked right past that table. I would have missed perhaps one of the biggest connections in my business life.

Winning entrepreneurs act in spite of how they feel. It's not always easy to do so. In fact, overcoming what we feel like doing versus what we should be doing is a daily battle in all areas of life, but it is a battle you must win. As you move forward toward your business goals, don't let your emotions cause you to miss a phenomenal, life-changing opportunity. If you do, you could be missing out on a lot of money.

78) Push beyond Your Fear

As soon as the fear approaches near, attack and destroy it.
—Chanakya, Indian philosopher

When I pulled through the grand entrance and saw the massive race track, I was overcome by a gripping fear. I could only see a few turns of the track, but the part I saw was enough to give me a shot of adrenaline, the kind that makes your stomach ache and gives you a metallic taste in your mouth. I had raced on smaller tracks, giving me an inflated sense of confidence, but this was the real deal, a challenging track used for professional and amateur sports car and motorcycle races.

That sunny Saturday morning, I arrived at Road Atlanta, a 2.54-mile track located about an hour north of Atlanta, Georgia. The track hosts the famous Petit Le Mans race, an annual sports car endurance race that draws over one hundred thousand fans. It was declared one of the best road courses in *Car and Driver* magazine in 2010. My client, Cadillac, invited me that day to their touring Cadillac V-Lab event, which allows VIP attendees to experience the 556 horsepower of the world's fastest luxury sedan, the Cadillac CTS-V.

After drag racing, short-course laps, and sessions on driving technique, the day culminated with racing on the track at full speed. My fear had subsided over the course of the day, but when our instructors summoned us to the pits, it returned with almost crippling intensity. The roaring engines and cars whipping past at speeds well over one hundred miles per hour fueled my anxiety. Nevertheless, I put on my face guard, grabbed my helmet, and found my game face.

What intimidated me most about the track, or at least the part I could see, were the elevation changes. They were visually terrifying. I would later find out that the elevation changes were the least of my worries. During my test run on the track, I encountered the track's famous or infamous "esses." I wasn't even going full speed, but I quickly lost my bearings and ended up running off the track. My instructor had to grab the wheel of the car to get me back on course. I was so embarrassed. From that point on, I was especially anxious, but eager to prove myself.

Nevertheless, I eventually recovered after a few more test runs and made a comeback. My fear gradually turned into excitement. On the straightaway part of the track, I reached 124 mph, a speed that I had never reached in a car on a race track. Despite running off the track earlier and allowing the esses to get to my psyche, I left my fear in the dust. I was able to complete a full-throttle run in a respectable time.

As I reflect on that exhilarating day, I realize that starting a business is similar in many ways. What it takes to be a successful race car driver is the perfect metaphor for what it takes to be a great entrepreneur. While you are excited for the journey ahead, you often must overcome your fears of failure and the unknown. The entrepreneurial path, just like a race track, has chicanes, undulating esses, tight hairpins, variations in elevation, and several twists and turns. All of these obstacles can cause fear.

But even if you are frightened and run off the road like I did, you push forward. You grab the wheel and step on the gas pedal, pushing through your inhibitions. Your commitment to the goal overcomes your trepidation, and that's what being an entrepreneur is all about.

79) Be a Maverick

Here's to the crazy ones. The rebels. The troublemakers. The ones who see things differently. While some may see them as the crazy ones, we see genius. Because the people who are crazy enough to think they can change the world, are the ones who do.
—Apple, "Think Different" campaign, advertising copy

It's no coincidence that several of the most successful and famous entrepreneurs were mavericks at a young age. You will also find that this rebellious nature is most evident during the teenage years and the early twenties, a time when young adults question the world in which they live and challenge the authorities that make the rules.

For instance, as fearless teenagers, the founders of Apple, Steve Jobs and Steve Wozniak, built and sold their illegal blue boxes for

$150 to customers who wanted to make long distance calls for free. Blue boxes were popular in the 1970s with drug dealers and other unsavory characters because they made tracing their phone calls impossible. In fact, Berkeley Blue and Oaf Tobark, the aliases that Wozniak and Jobs used, respectively, to conduct their illegal business actually were robbed at gunpoint when trying to sell their blue box to a shady prospect. Jobs was quoted as saying that Apple would never have existed if he and his best friend, Wozniak, had not gone through their blue-box experience. Perhaps being threatened with a pistol motivated them to conduct business on the stock market, not the black market.

Fast-forward about twenty-five years. Two other mavericks who would also change the world as we know it were up to no good. The founders of a new search engine called BackRub were busy casing the loading dock at Stanford University's computer science building. The two students were stealing new computers that were delivered to the computer science department for use in the students' own search engine project that needed more computing power. The two thieves were Sergey Brin and Larry Page, the founders of Google. According to their professors, this irreverence for the computer science department's property was not shocking. Brin and Page often challenged their professors, frequently calling them "bastards." Apparently, not even the possibility of arrest was enough to stop these two mavericks—or processor pirates—from pursuing their idea.

Just a few years later I found myself in college, unknowingly continuing the tradition of rebellious young techies who transform their mischievous energy into entrepreneurial genius. I certainly wasn't selling products to gangster-like characters or stealing computers from my computer science department, but I did manage to undermine the communications system of my college by creating my own more popular system. Students had more confidence in my web-based system than the school's system, which was often offline due to networking problems. In fact, I had so much power that the president of my college summoned me to his office to have a talk with me. I created my system in part because the school turned down my proposal to create web-based software that would facilitate student communication and would move telephone registration to online registration. Creating my own system was my way of getting them back for rejecting me. This experience served as the basis for my eventual desire to be an entrepreneur and to create my own company.

As mavericks grow older, their rebellious nature stays with them and is a significant contributor to their entrepreneurial success. What we know as teenage rebellion often becomes industry disruption, a new way of doing things that upsets those who support the status quo. These mavericks go on to change the world. If you ever needed a reason to tap into your desire to be a rebel, you have one now.

80) Make Your Dreams Come True

All our dreams can come true, if we have the courage to pursue them.
—Walt Disney, founder, the Walt Disney Company

As he approached the middle of the basketball court, Michael Jordan had tears in his eyes. It was halftime during his final NBA All-Star Game in 2003, a highly emotional moment for sports fans around the world. Amid thunderous applause and with a packed Philips Arena in Atlanta, Georgia, Jordan waved to the cheering fans and cherished the special moment. After a long standing ovation, he humbly said, "To all the fans who supported the game of basketball, not just Michael Jordan. I thank you for your support. I leave the game in good hands. . . . Now I can go home and feel at peace with the game of basketball." I was there in person and had a front-row seat to history in the making.

Growing up in Harrisburg, Pennsylvania, from age six to about eleven years old, all I did was play and watch basketball. My friends and I all wanted to go to the NBA. We were obsessed. I loved basketball so much that my father paid a good sum of money to pave our backyard with asphalt and erect a regulation basketball hoop. My older brother and I played out there most of the year—in freezing snow and in one-hundred-plus-degree weather. I played in every league that I could during every season. I religiously did my basketball drills in my basement (basketball fans remember the spider dribble and figure-eight drills). I was determined to live up to my namesake and make it to the pros . . . until I stopped growing at five-feet-nine.

When I stopped growing, I started studying. With the same passion I once played basketball, I studied math and science. While a junior in high school, I received a full scholarship compliments of NASA to attend Morehouse College in Atlanta and study computer science. Even though trying to make it to the NBA was never about chasing money, I now understood that I would have to make my millions in technology instead of bouncing a ball. While in college I figured out that entrepreneurship was the ideal path for me to follow. Building my business gave me the same exciting and fulfilling feeling that playing basketball gave me when I was younger.

Just three years after I started my company, the NBA approached me to help promote its 2003 All-Star Game in Atlanta. My company had done work with the Atlanta Hawks franchise the year before, and the Hawks marketing department recommended my company to the NBA when it sought reputable local companies to partner with during the All-Star Game. The NBA hired my company to market the 2003 weekend and to help make it a huge success. I was especially thrilled because not only was my dream as a kid to play in the NBA, but I also wanted to attend the three-point contest and exciting slam-dunk contest. Here was my chance to do so.

During that weekend, I had the opportunity to be around many of my sports heroes, including Magic Johnson, Michael Jordan, Kobe Bryant, Isaiah Thomas, Shaquille O'Neil, and many more.

Celebrities were hanging out, too. Nick Cannon, Ashton Kutcher, Nelly, and others were there. But there was no experience like the NBA All-Star Game itself. Because I had an extra ticket to the game, I invited my dad to go with me. He booked a flight from Chicago and joined me for one of the most exciting times of my life, and all due to my entrepreneurial efforts.

Even though I have never played in an NBA game, my dream to work for the NBA still came true. It just turned out to be different than what I expected. Instead of the NBA paying me to play basketball, it pays me to plan some of its marketing strategy and tactics. Instead of sitting on the bench as a player (where I would probably be), I sit courtside as a spectator. To this day, the NBA continues as one of my best clients, and the dream continues. Entrepreneurs make their dreams happen in many ways, and my experience is a testament to that. Who knows? Maybe one day I will get to own an NBA franchise. How cool would that be!

81) Make Difficult Sacrifices

Great achievement is usually born of great sacrifice.
—Napoleon Hill, author, *Think and Grow Rich*

Knowing he was a husband and a recent father, I asked an acquaintance, "How are your wife and newborn son?" He hesitated before answering, and then he replied with a blank, emotionless face, "I got a divorce." I was caught off guard by his candid response. What I thought was a cordial inquiry suddenly turned into an awkward social moment. I can't remember exactly what I said afterward, but my new friend continued talking about how his divorce was the right decision. Apparently, he and his ex-wife had a major disagreement about his entrepreneurial drive and his need to be in Silicon Valley thousands of miles away from the East Coast. He talked about how he must go for the "billion-dollar idea" in order to leave his son a legacy. When he spoke I could tell that he was convinced that he was making the right decision. Only time will tell.

After my conversation with a well-known Silicon Valley entrepreneur, I thought about my own willingness to make difficult sacrifices in the name of chasing a big dream. A new husband and father myself, I can't imagine leaving my wife and young son to pursue a new business on the other side of the country. The thought would never cross my mind. I wondered, if I were ever that convicted by the promise of a billion-dollar idea or a once-in-a-lifetime opportunity, would I sacrifice my marriage and a relationship with my son? And, if I could, would I be able to live with myself? The answer is an emphatic no, but I know my wife, and she supports what I do 100 percent.

Such is the life of a dedicated entrepreneur who understands that in order to reach goals, there will be sacrifices, some small and some large. Most entrepreneurs are willing to make small sacrifices. For example, giving up a few good meals for the proverbial ramen noodles is almost a rite of passage for the struggling entrepreneur. (I've certainly had my share of ramen noodles and wonder if there is a correlation between being an entrepreneur and having high blood pressure.) However, when it comes to making big sacrifices like giving up a high-paying job, a college education, good health, a family, and other important things, the dynamics of the discussion change. There seems to be a split between regular entrepreneurs, who sacrifice little, and extreme entrepreneurs, who sacrifice a lot.

In general, you can measure how badly an entrepreneur wants an idea to become reality based on what that person is willing to sacrifice. Accordingly, one's level of success is directly related to sacrifice. Keeping this in mind, I often ask prospective cofounders and staff for my companies what they are willing to give up to be part of a winning team. They frequently give the expected answer: "I would give my right arm!" But the fruits of their labor can be found in the pains of their sacrifice. I can surmise the real answer before I ask the question by looking at what they have accomplished already and what they have suffered to do it.

Entrepreneurs have to sacrifice as they chase their dreams. However, rarely do we discuss just how hard these sacrifices will be to reach high levels of success. We joke about eating ramen noodles because it's trivial. But would you leave a high-paying job? Would you drop out of college even if you had a full scholarship? Would you give up your health? Would you sacrifice your marriage and a relationship with your son? Extreme entrepreneurs say yes to difficult questions like these, and that's what makes entrepreneurs a rare breed. As you embark on your journey to bring your big idea to the world, ask yourself the question, *What am I willing to sacrifice to make this happen?* Your answer can help you determine your likelihood of success.

82) You Have Unbelievable Endurance

Endurance is one of the most difficult disciplines, but it is to the one who endures that the final victory comes.
—Siddhartha Gautama, Indian philosopher, founder of Buddhism

If you want to know what it's like to run a business, then run a marathon—seriously. Training for and running a marathon is the closest experience to starting and running a business. Interestingly, it turns out that not only are the two experiences extremely similar, but they also share a statistic that makes their likeness even more compelling.

Recently, my curiosity inspired me to investigate how many people run a marathon (26.2 miles) or a half marathon (13.1 miles) annually and how many people start a business annually. In 2010, for example, approximately 1.9 million people finished marathons or half marathons, according to Running USA. That's less than 1 percent of the U.S. population. Likewise, in 2010, 340 out of every 100,000 adults started a business, according to the Kauffman

Foundation. After adding the nonadult population back to the population figure to make the comparison more accurate, that's a rate of less than 1 percent of the U.S. population. Roughly the same percentage of those who put themselves through the challenging experience of running a marathon or a half marathon take the difficult plunge to start a business. One reason: Both are extreme in that they attract individuals who have a high tolerance for pain. Put another way, both require unbelievable endurance.

Inspired by my older brother, an extreme runner who has run around the world once and across the United States twice, I began running half marathons in 2008. Considering how fast my brother was, I had high hopes for my performance. I thought my four-year advantage in age would give me an edge, so I set my goal high from the start. I wanted to finish the half in 1 hour, 45 minutes. Well, let's just say that I haven't reached that goal. I didn't think it would be easy to beat that time, but I sure didn't think it would be as hard. During my first race, I injured my leg at about mile 9 because I was running too fast, and I didn't train properly. My time was 2:14:33. After that race, I adjusted my goal to breaking 2 hours. It would take me four races and over three years to reach that goal. In January 2012 I not only broke two hours but I also crushed my goal time, finishing the race in 1:54:10. I beat my next best time by a huge 10 minutes, a long time in long-distance running. Reflecting on my personal best, I could trace the momentous achievement to my increased endurance training.

Since taking up running in 2008, I've learned firsthand that running long distances and running a business have many elements in common. Of the similarities, the most compelling is certainly the need to have tremendous endurance in both to be successful. The need for endurance shows up in many different aspects of each endeavor.

When you are finally running the marathon, you have times when you just want to give up. You are overwhelmed by the long distance ahead or by how tired your body is. Sometimes I think to myself, *Why on Earth am I doing this? What do I have to prove? Wouldn't it be great to stop and rest?* In the same way, when you are running a business, sometimes you want to throw in the towel. You may be losing money, trying to build a working prototype, or dealing with a legal battle. You may say to yourself, *Having a job is so much easier.* Despite these roadblocks, you keep the end goal in mind and push through the difficulties, settling in on a good pace.

Also, the more you run, the better you become. After the terrible performance of my first race, my brother told me that I'll get better the more I run. I thought he said this just to cheer me up, but he was right. The more I ran, the more I understood how my body reacts to different types of environments and training regimens. I learned how to avoid injury, what weather conditions I prefer, and how to maximize my workouts. I also received advice from elite runners on how to train, what to eat, and what brand of clothes, shoes, and socks to wear. It made a huge difference in my performance and endurance. Likewise, the more businesses you start or the longer you are in business, the better you become. In fact, according to a Harvard University study, first-time entrepreneurs have only an 18 percent chance of succeeding; entrepreneurs who previously failed have a 20 percent chance of succeeding.

Moreover, long-term and consistent training properly prepares you for top performance. Running a marathon is not something that you decide to do on a whim the day or week before. It requires the commitment to train and to withstand the arduous preparation for the big run. Beginners need about eighteen weeks to train for a full marathon and about twelve weeks for a half marathon. If the distance itself doesn't deter people from running a marathon, than training almost every day of the week for months will do it. Similarly, if you start a business without any training, you will make many mistakes you could have avoided completely. To prepare for business, your training regimen involves attending conferences, reading books and magazines, and finding a mentor.

More than any other characteristic of an entrepreneur, having superhuman endurance is by far the most vital. It's even more important than being smart, well-funded, or charismatic. Entrepreneurs who have the fortitude to keep going despite being tired, to continue to educate themselves to be top performers, and to work through long-lasting pain are the most likely to find success. Many people say that running a business is like running a marathon. Having done both, I certainly agree.

83) Be Prepared to Lose It All

If I didn't make it in this world, I would probably be homeless. I gave myself that little to fall back on.
—Shawn Wayans, actor, producer

I sat alone in my apartment staring at the wall in front of me. I wondered how I was going to make ends meet. My company wasn't making any money at the time, and my pride prevented me from asking for help. I was at an all-time low, and I had no one to talk to about it. I felt miserable and extremely lonely.

During the next few days, I carried on as usual and hung out with friends to try and lighten my spirits. I was good at hiding my feelings of despair. Besides, I felt like I had to act normally because my friends and family thought I was rich. They had no clue that I could barely pay my rent and other basic bills. If I had mentioned my financial struggles, they wouldn't have believed me. In their opinion, I was one of the many young dotcom superstars prevalent in the media during the time. In other words, they thought that I was well-off enough to retire at the age of twenty-one. They would never believe that I was on the verge of losing it all, including my own mind.

I eventually overcame my low point, but it was a difficult learning experience. It was the first of a few times when I felt like giving up because the pressure and stress were so great. However, each crucible has prepared me to better deal with challenging times. Despite the emotional strain and tremendous stress, I was determined to remain an entrepreneur. Every time, I was able to come out on top and to grow more comfortable with my ability to avert disaster, but it doesn't always happen that way for everybody.

Rarely do entrepreneurs talk about how bad times can get. If we do talk about them, we gloss over them, minimizing and maybe even making light of the experiences. We joke about eating ramen noodles or peanut butter and jelly sandwiches. We laugh about not having any money to pay bills or messing up our credit. All of these experiences are much easier to talk about once they have passed, and we find ourselves in a position of relative comfort.

Instead of avoiding the difficult conversation or glossing over it, remember every now and then just how depressing times can get. Contrary to popular and glorified belief, even as an entrepreneur you sometimes won't know where your next dollar is coming from. You may consider filing bankruptcy. You may feel like you have to role-play among friends and family who admire your entrepreneurial courage and envy your fictitious bank account. You'll have days when you just want to curl up in a ball and sleep your worries away. In the pursuit of their business dreams, entrepreneurs have sacrificed marriages, family time, financial stability, health, and the list goes on.

While I will always be an entrepreneur and I tout the many wonderful reasons I choose to be an entrepreneur, I know that this is the hardest thing that I have ever done in my life. I also know that a lot of what we see in the media is hype. Not every entrepreneur is making lots of money and living the perfect life. At no point do I want to give people a one-sided view of entrepreneurship, because it's not reality. Entrepreneurship is not for the weak. If you aren't prepared to lose it all, then you should definitely do something else.

Chapter 7

Motivation

People often say that *motivation* doesn't last. Well, neither
does *bathing*—that's why we recommend it daily.
—Zig Ziglar, author, motivational speaker

The word "motivation" in a business context often con-
jures up images of a room full of corporate managers getting an expensive pep talk from motivational speakers
like Zig Ziglar and Les Brown. But motivation comes in several
different forms, many of which are subtle and even subconscious.
As an entrepreneur, you must be keenly aware of what motivates
you to ensure that your maximum effort is sustainable.

In this chapter, you learn about what motivates the most successful entrepreneurs, ranging from getting fired to wanting to create the best possible product on the market. You learn some of the
signs—some of which may surprise you—that your motivation is
well-placed or misplaced. Hopefully, these stories, statistics, and
beliefs are motivational in themselves. Ultimately, you should
align your motivation with your business goals, a challenging but
attainable feat.

---

84) Being Successful Is Not the Goal

Nothing recedes like success.
—Walter Winchell, newspaper and radio gossip commentator

In 2009, Canadian recording artist Drake released "Successful," the second single from his third release, titled *So Far Gone*. The song has a melodic and a catchy chorus: "I just wanna be, I just wanna be successful." The same lyric is repeated over and over as if it were a religious chant. Drake glorifies what he believes is the life of a successful person, craving money, cars, women, clothes, and awards. As I heard the song for the first time, I certainly could relate to the twenty-three-year-old's desire to be successful. But as someone seven years his senior I couldn't help to think how being successful is such a frivolous goal and how desiring accolades, possessions, and cheap companionship won't bring long-lasting joy.

I often mentor or cross paths with people who think that being an entrepreneur is one of the fastest ways to become successful or to gain respect. They see the media frenzy surrounding Facebook's IPO or Instagram's billion-dollar acquisition; they watch their favorite music artists and actors in the limelight, making millions of dollars. The pressure to be respected by peers and to live a successful lifestyle is especially prevalent among members of generation Y. In fact, according to a recent study from the University of Oregon, the desire for respect as a core value has risen tremendously over the levels of previous years. The study's lead author, Eda Gurel-Atay, said, "We found that people want respect for themselves and they want to be important to other people." This increased value is quite evident in social media, as the heightened desire for respect and importance often turns into embellished and narcissistic posts on Facebook. Unfortunately, the motivation of these posts, like Drake's song, is a belief that true success comes from status, not from self-actualization.

211

A true entrepreneur is not driven by outward appearances of success, but rather by solving a problem whose solution provides value to its customers. This dedication shows up time and time again among high achievers in business, and it's most evident among those who despite their great wealth and accomplishments continue to live a modest lifestyle. For example, Mark Zuckerberg, CEO of Facebook, was a renter for years even though he was worth billions of dollars. His commitment to Facebook's original goal of enhancing human communication was reiterated in his speech on the day his company went public: "Our mission isn't to be a public company. Our mission is to make the world more open and connected." He could have cashed out years ago, but his concept of being successful is making his idea a complete reality, or in other words, attaining self-actualization.

Many serial entrepreneurs learn the value of self-actualization after the first exit. After reaching a point in my life where I thought I was successful, this feeling didn't last very long. Although other people continued to think I was successful, I didn't go on feeling that way. I had sold my first company and was off to starting the next one. I learned that what matters most to me isn't so much receiving the rewards of a highly profitable company as much as it is solving problems, building valuable companies, and making an impact in the world. Yes, it may sound lofty, but it's the reason I get up every morning and the measure by which I determine my success.

There's nothing wrong with wanting to be successful, but it is the wrong reason to start a business. Starting a business to be successful is like getting married to have sex. People too often focus on the benefits of the undertaking rather than the true purpose. If you remember to focus on your purpose—unadulterated by any ulterior motives—you stay headed in the right direction to accomplish your goal, and the benefits of your efforts are more likely to accrue to you. I like how Dave Navarro, "the Launch Coach," put it: "Success is not a person. It's an event."

85) You Are Excited When Monday Morning Arrives

> It's just another manic Monday
> I wish it were Sunday
> 'Cause that's my funday
> My I-don't-have-to-runday
> It's just another manic Monday
> —Lyrics from "Manic Monday," The Bangles

"Manic Monday," the catchy song that debuted in 1986 by American pop rock band the Bangles and written by Prince, describes the weekly angst of so many people who get up to go to work on a Monday morning. Although I was only six years old in 1986, I remember the song's melody well and can still recite some of the lyrics by heart. As a toddler, I had no idea what the song meant. I just knew there was something peculiar about a Monday. Soon enough, though, I was able to relate to the song: Just a few months later, Monday morning meant time to go to school, and that's no more fun than having to go to work.

The Bangles's song became a hit because so many people could relate to it. Everyone at some point in life has had Monday morning woes. While the song describes a common anxiety in a fun, lighthearted way, the matter of Monday mania is much more serious than you might think.

A disproportionate number of heart attacks occur on Monday mornings. The reason? People are so stressed out about going to work on Monday that their blood pressure levels skyrocket, increasing the likelihood of a heart attack. A study conducted by Japan's Tokyo Women's Medical University and published in the *American Journal of Hypertension* in 2005 proves that having a job can be devastating to your health. So much for the matter being lighthearted!

In contrast to this gloomy and depressing reality for millions of Americans, one group of people actually loves Monday mornings.

These people neither have a theme song written by a huge rock star nor a published medical study about how little stress they have. Who are these rare people? Entrepreneurs. Entrepreneurs love Mondays. Why? Several reasons, but here are two of my favorites:

1. *Mondays represent a rebirth.* Working on a Monday is like hitting the reset button. Most entrepreneurs work nonstop, so Mondays—if for no other reason than being the first workday of the week—represent a time to restart and to refocus.

2. *Mondays are business as usual.* On Monday, the world seems to be functioning in its totality once again. People are back in their offices. They return calls. They return e-mails. Because it's an official workday, people feel more obligated to get back to you. And if you are in sales or negotiations, nothing is worse than the weekend killing your momentum. You can't conquer the world if it stops for two days.

Those of you who are already entrepreneurs probably nod your heads in agreement. On the other hand, those of you who are working a 9-to-5 and have entrepreneurial dreams find it hard to believe that anyone would love a Monday morning. This segment is for you. But don't worry about actively trying to assume this characteristic. It's automatic.

An entrepreneur who dreads Mondays is probably not an entrepreneur for the right reasons. If you need a litmus test to see if your motivation is where it needs to be, this is it. Put another way, if you are an entrepreneur and you don't like Mondays, it's probably time to do something else. How you feel on this critical day is so important. After all, it could be a matter of life or death—literally.

86) You're Disappointed When Friday Arrives

> I hate weekends because there is no stock market.
> —Rene Rivkin, Australian stockbroker, entrepreneur

A few months ago on a Monday morning, I updated my Facebook status with the following: "I absolutely love Mondays. Not so thrilled about Fridays." I anticipated some lighthearted criticism from my friends, but I didn't think that my sanity would be questioned. One of my neighbors commented, "You are crazy, man." I didn't take offense, though. As shocking and direct as his comment was, he had a point.

While most people understand why I love Mondays, they don't understand why I dislike Fridays. They think that everyone loves Fridays. Even if you work for yourself or run a business, Friday is the day that ends the arduous workweek, signaling leisure time for going to parties, sleeping in, working out, running errands, spending time with family, and doing many other things that are fun. How could you not like Fridays, right?

The joy of Friday is ingrained in our culture. For example, countless songs are about Friday and its happy significance. Perhaps the most popular is "Friday on My Mind" by the Easybeats, an Australian rock-and-roll band from the 1960s. The lyrics of the song include this sentiment, "Nothing else that bugs me more than workin' for the rich man." For both the writer of this lyric and millions of disgruntled workers, Friday represents freedom, albeit temporary, from the man. Likewise, we have expressions like T.G.I.F. (Thank God/Goodness It's Friday), after which a popular chain of restaurants is named. Happy hours are especially lively on Fridays. Anything less than praise for Fridays and all they represent is darn near sacrilegious. For some, Friday is more sacred than the Sabbath.

Well, the Friday worshippers will just have to burn me at the stake, because I am the anti-Friday. Fridays are my hell. I am especially tetchy on that day, and my morale is low. Sometimes I even go several hours without eating. I am exhausted trying to motivate team members who have their mind on dashing out of the office. I am simply a depressed mess.

I find that other entrepreneurs are like me on Fridays for numerous reasons; three are common. First, *Friday is in large part a useless day*. Employee productivity goes way down. According to a survey by Accountemps, a staffing and temp agency, Fridays are the least productive day of the workweek by far. No surprise here. Second, *it's payday*—for everybody else. There's no stress like having trouble meeting payroll. While everyone is feeling like a fat cat, you feel like a skinny dog. Third, *you have to wait an entire two days to get anything done*. Most entrepreneurs are always working. That's the life we choose and love, but it's especially frustrating when you have those same unrealistic and demanding expectations for everyone else.

Friday might as well be "Cryday." And there is no happy hour, just "unhappy hour." Such are the lives of entrepreneurs, full of strange dichotomies: We like Mondays while everyone else likes Fridays; we like to work while everyone else plays; we write checks while everyone else gets paid. Don't get me wrong. I am not complaining. In fact, I think my Facebook friend was right. I *am* crazy. But I like being crazy—crazy rich, that is, even if it means hating Fridays.

87) A 9-to-5 Is Worse Than Death

A real job is a job you hate.
—Bill Watterson, cartoonist, author

Every day, to make ends meet, millions of Americans go to a job they hate. Every day, I make ends meet to avoid going to a job I would hate. While the average employee hopes he never gets fired, I hope I never get hired. Most employees have to fight just to get a small raise; I am an entrepreneur because it makes no sense to place a limit on my income. Many people find self-worth in employment; I find self-worth in entrepreneurship. This is my reality, and although it's not normal, I think it's most natural.

Don't get me wrong. I have much respect for people who do what it takes to earn an income to support themselves or their family. I can somewhat relate. I have worked some jobs that were terrible—for me, anyway. For example, I once worked a seasonal job at Macy's, and I thought I was going to die. I had to get up at 4:30 a.m. to sell watches and push consumer credit cards, standing all day and pleasing some of the most discourteous customers. Each day I came home wondering how people did this type of work for years. Having to stand and watch the time all day seemed like cruel and unusual punishment, not a job. When the Christmas season ended, I was eager to return to my old self.

As ridiculous as it sounds, I actually have a very real fear of having to work a 9-to-5. In fact, I fear it more than death itself. The fear is so intense that I often have nightmares about it. Upon further analysis of my fear, a trained psychologist would probably determine that I am not scared about a job per se. Instead, I am more terrified of failure. The job is just an outward sign of what would be a crushing inner defeat. Having a job would mean that I was unable to continue my life as an entrepreneur full-time, doing what I find most fulfilling. In this respect, I am like everyone else who rates fear of failure as one of their biggest phobias.

We often hear the popular phrase "No fear!" In fact, it's a popular selling t-shirt. The phenomenon is a great example of how our culture glorifies an unattainable reality in which we fear nothing. Fear is the ultimate enemy that we must conquer. Well, I beg to differ. In some cases, fear is good. If, like I do, you fear having a 9-to-5 job, you are motivated to do all you can to avoid it. So far, things have worked out well for me.

Entrepreneurs are often touted for being fearless. This perception is not reality, though. Entrepreneurs are human and have fears like everyone else. Most likely, having a job is one of those fears, but we just channel that fear into something constructive like motivation or the courage to excel. When healthy fear is combined with a greater desire to succeed, nothing can stop you.

88) Your Parents Want You to Get a Real Job with Benefits

My son is now an "entrepreneur." That's what you're called when you don't have a job.
—Ted Turner, founder, CNN; businessman; philanthropist

It was too late. How could I have been so careless and left the letter sitting on my bureau? My mother, whose curiosity often has no regard for her children's privacy, had the letter in her hand. I don't think that she read the whole thing before sprinting to show it to my father. I am almost sure she stopped reading around the third paragraph of the two-page letter that stated, "Your initial compensation will be $55,000 per year. . . . If you decide to accept employment with us, we will pay you a signing bonus in the amount of $5,000 payable upon acceptance." Oh no! My parents found out what I had hoped they never would.

That Christmas holiday in 2000, I was barely a senior in college and had just turned twenty years old. Three weeks before I went home for the break, I received an offer letter from one of the then Big 5 consulting firms, but hadn't read it. I was not interested in reading it, because I had no intention of actually taking the job—no matter how much money the company offered me. Over the holiday, I finally decided to read the letter. The package was worth over $80,000 in 2012 dollars, not including benefits.

The first thing that my father said to me after finding out about the job offer took me by surprise. He grumbled, "Even after working for the same company for over thirty years, I don't even get twenty days of paid vacation." After his comment, I felt a bit guilty for having blown off the offer. I knew after that awkward encounter that he and my mother wanted me to accept the offer, which symbolized the summation of all their efforts. I felt like the golden child. I had received a full ride to college, and now I had an incredible job offer during what pundits said was one of the worst job markets for college graduates in years. Still, I wanted to take a different path, a more exciting adventure that I thought would lead me to true self-actualization.

My parents eventually accepted my decision to pursue entrepreneurship 100 percent. After that Christmas holiday they never really pushed me get a "real job." I thank them for that. Perhaps their support comes from having full confidence in me to accomplish my goals. I suppose it helped, too, that I was able to take care of myself from day one with little help from them. The funny thing is that nowadays my mother, who still believes that a corporate job is the highest form of security and social prestige, often asks me with a tone of motherly concern, "How is your business?" As I have during the last twelve years, I reassure her, saying, "It's going well." For some reason, I don't think my answer lessens her concern, especially since I have a family now. My dad doesn't say much, although I know he's supportive.

If your parents want you to get a real job, be patient with them. Of course, they have your best interest at heart. I am just over thirty years old, and I think they would still like for me to get a real job. It's just the expectation of their generation, and anything outside the norm is a huge risk. In many ways, they are right. We all know that more businesses fail than succeed. As for you, the best thing to do is to work hard to build a business that is profitable and highly successful. Perhaps write them a check every now and then. How can they not be proud of that?

In case you were wondering what company offered me the job, it was Arthur Andersen, the consulting firm that no longer exists. The firm went down with Enron in one of the largest accounting scandals and financial disasters in history. Enron declared bankruptcy on December 2, 2001. Had I accepted their offer I would have been unemployed in just a few months.

In another strange twist of fate, my father was recently forced into semiretirement by a company for which he'd worked for almost forty years. The company let him and other highly experienced executives go in a less than honorable way that not even he could have imagined. Who knows? Maybe this is a good thing. Now I can encourage him to become an entrepreneur.

89) You Sometimes Get More Resentment Than Respect

Entrepreneurs are the forgotten heroes of America.
—Ronald Reagan, fortieth president, United States of America

When you become an entrepreneur, you don't receive a superhero outfit with a big "E" on the front of it. Although you are indeed superhuman—having taken an ocean-sized leap that many would never consider, having solved complex problems, and having turned a passion into profit—the ordinary person doesn't value your superpowers. And when you become successful, Gotham won't throw you a party to thank you for helping to save the economy; it will probably just send you a higher tax bill. To most people, you are the same person you always were. You are far from being a superhero on an elite team like the Avengers, fighting and squashing unemployment, recessions, and underdevelopment. In fact, some people consider you to be more like a villain than a savior.

Part of the recent blame for this lack of appreciation is the poor economy. Entrepreneurship has now been proposed as the panacea for our economic ills. As more and more economists and government officials believe that encouraging entrepreneurship at its basic level is a partial solution to getting our economy going again, entrepreneurship has lost some of its prestige and allure. It has become a romantic, bureaucratic last resort to help people who have no jobs. In a few states, programs to spur entrepreneurship appear just as the reserves for unemployment benefits near depletion. Sadly, it has come to this: Being an entrepreneur has become a euphemism for being unemployed. Being an entrepreneur has even been associated with being lazy. Instead of entrepreneurship being a badge of accomplishment, it has become a stigma of shame. The good thing is that this attitude will likely change as the economy improves, but people resent entrepreneurs for two other long-standing reasons.

1. *Jealousy is perhaps the most common reason that entrepreneurs do not get the respect they deserve*, especially from people close to them. As if watching an embellished Facebook feed, resentful spectators are envious of some entrepreneurs' amazing lifestyles. They don't see the hard work that goes into making that lifestyle possible. It takes superhero-like confidence and gumption to become an entrepreneur—and everyone knows this. Entrepreneurs are extremely rare, comprising less than 1 percent of the overall U.S. population. Despite these facts, people are always jealous of those who take the risks to do something great, and jealousy often manifests itself as resentment.

2. *Entrepreneurs receive disrespect because they are no longer on the corporate grid or part of the matrix*. As a result, people cannot necessarily put them into a nice box labeled "lawyer," "mechanic," or "secretary." For them, there is an unsettling mystery about what entrepreneurs do, how they spend their time, where they go, and so on. They wonder how they make ends meet. People who are class conscious especially have difficulty because they have no idea how much money an entrepreneur makes. They want to discover who makes more money so that they can assuage the anxiety of their curiosity. In general, people are afraid of and dismissive of what they don't understand or know; unfortunately, that includes entrepreneurs.

An upside is that entrepreneurs who encounter such resentment often turn it into a powerful motivator. In the same way that a superhero may be motivated to disprove a naysayer, an entrepreneur is inspired to silence resentment toward entrepreneurship, and even personal attacks. Superheroes and entrepreneurs do what must be done regardless. Ultimately, they know that resentment and respect are not mutually exclusive.

90) It's Not about Being Your Own Boss

"Kill my boss? Do I dare live out the American Dream?"
—Homer Simpson, in *The Simpsons*

For a moment, it seemed as if the message was everywhere—on television, on radio, in countless Twitter and Facebook messages. Every day, I heard someone or saw some advertisement touting the greatest benefit of entrepreneurship. What was this great benefit? Well, it wasn't how pursuing entrepreneurship can possibly make you wealthy. Nor was it that entrepreneurship is the key to true independence. Instead, entrepreneurship enables you to "be your own boss." How lame! Above all, how deceiving!

This clever pitch appeals to those who have a job and want to escape from their boss, but can't. That would be like persuading a prisoner to break out of jail because then he could be his own warden. Why would you want to be your own boss, someone you despise?

Being your own boss is not the right reason to pursue entrepreneurship for two reasons.

1. *The phrase "being your own boss" appeals to those who believe that a domineering boss is a bad thing.* They crave the freedom to do what they want when they want. People with this attitude generally make terrible entrepreneurs. As many entrepreneurs will tell you, unless you have strong self-discipline, a demanding boss figure that keeps you on track to success is a great thing,

whether it's yourself, an investor, a mentor, or a board. One thing is for sure: In order to be a successful entrepreneur, discipline is a must. There is no escaping it.

2. *The misguided "be your own boss" pitch appeals to a false idea of what being an entrepreneur means.* It implies that to be an entrepreneur is to be a manager. Not true. Author and entrepreneurial guru Michael Gerber put it best in his classic book, *The E Myth.* He explains that three types of people go into business: the entrepreneur, the manager, and the technician. Gerber writes,

> The entrepreneurial personality turns the most trivial condition into an exceptional opportunity. The Entrepreneur is the visionary in us. The dreamer. The energy behind every human activity. The energy that sparks the fire of the future. The catalyst for change . . . to the entrepreneur, most people are problems that get in the way of the dream.

On the other hand, a boss or The Manager is pragmatic. Gerber continues, "Without The Manager there would be no planning, no order, no predictability. . . . Without The Manager, there could be no business, no society." An entrepreneur is not a manager.

I would be much happier if those "be your own boss" ads never mentioned entrepreneurship. Ideally, they would proclaim, "Own your own business!" and stop there. The Entrepreneur, as Gerber puts it, "builds a house and the instant it's done begins planning the next one." Entrepreneurs aren't interested in being bosses at all, and if an entrepreneur has to be a boss, this role is most certainly temporary.

People who subscribe to the be-your-own-boss fallacy cripple their entrepreneurial potential and are in it for the wrong reason. Are you a boss or an entrepreneur?

91) Entrepreneurship Is in Your Blood, Literally

Inspiration comes from all different places.
—Jeffrey Katzenberg, CEO, DreamWorks Animation

Oprah Winfrey is known for making guests on her show cry. However, this time, she was the one who would shed tears, overcome by the significance and serendipity of the moment.

In 2007 I stumbled upon a television special titled *Oprah's Roots: An African American Lives Special*, in which producer Henry Louis Gates Jr. revealed shocking news to Winfrey about her family history. Gates, head of Harvard's Afro-American Studies program, researched Winfrey's family history extensively and decided to share what he found in a television special. The revelation was astonishing.

Gates shared that Winfrey's great-great-grandfather, a former slave, bought a large amount of land and built on it a school for African American children. Considering the times, this achievement was extraordinary. When Winfrey learned this amazing piece of history, she was speechless. Tears came to her eyes. A blank stare turned into a confident smile. Winfrey, whose passions are education and land, instantly made the connection to her trailblazing ancestor. Like him, she built a school for young children and owns quite a bit of land. Oprah found renewed meaning and validation of her purpose in life. (Coincidentally, my wife and I went horseback riding on Winfrey's land in Hana, Hawaii, in 2008. We learned then that her land there was one of several properties that she owns around the world.)

While watching the television special, I couldn't help but get emotional, too. I felt tremendous joy for Winfrey and hope for myself that someday I would find someone in my family who was a trailblazing entrepreneur. As a young entrepreneur I struggled to find positive affirmation from my family that entrepreneurship was an honorable and legitimate path. Having a network of friends and associates who are entrepreneurs is wonderful, but having support-ive family members—extended or immediate—makes a difference.

My older brother was the closest to an entrepreneur. Having graduated from Berklee College of Music in Boston and traveled the world playing jazz piano with Wynton Marsalis and Herbie Hancock, he was in charge of finding his band's gigs, booking the band, and paying band members. He created a company through which he produced his CDs and managed his piano-tuning ap-pointments. Other than my brother, no one in my immediate family was close to being an entrepreneur. On both sides of my extended family, everyone worked a normal 9-to-5 job.

I would later find out just how rare entrepreneurs are. Accord-ing to the Kauffman Foundation, Atlanta ranked second among top metro areas in 2011 in the creation of new business. In 2011, 500 out of 100,000 adults ages twenty to sixty-four started a business. Los Angeles was the top city with 580 out of 100,000. That's ap-proximately 0.58 percent in the most entrepreneurial city in the United States. No wonder it's so hard to find a family member who's an entrepreneur.

My paternal grandmother was born in 1912. I never thought that she would be the link to connect me to relatives who owned their own businesses. When encouraging my siblings and me to watch a video of my grandmother talking about her life, my father men-tioned that she had a brother who owned a grocery store. After ask-ing my dad to tell me more, I learned that my uncle Thomas and uncle Dan were my enterprising great-uncles. Uncle Thomas would deliver groceries with his horse and buggy, while Uncle Dan would make trips to the coal mines in Pennsylvania to collect coal to sell in Baltimore. After learning this, I didn't come to tears like Oprah, but I searched for and found a connection. I wasn't so odd after all.

Choosing to be an entrepreneur can be a lonely endeavor and experience, especially if no one in your family is one. But I en-courage you to do a little research on your family, and chances are you will find someone who took the same risks that you did. Just like Oprah Winfrey and me, you will find that one brave family member who gives you extra inspiration and makes you proud. As the character Charlotte Phelan said in the Academy Award–winning movie *The Help*, "Courage sometimes skips a generation."

92) You Know Your Worth

Self-worth comes from one thing—thinking that you are worthy.
—Wayne Dyer, self-help author, motivational speaker

John looked me square in the eyes and with a stern face and faint whisper shared a disturbing secret. His revelation threw me for a loop. He warned, "They hire and pay very well the computer science majors who go to Georgia Tech. All the interns from other schools are paid lower wages and given lower positions. Many of them are just happy to be here, so they work for free or take crumbs. Don't let that happen to you. Make sure they pay you what you're worth." John was a veteran intern with the company and a senior at Georgia Tech. His information was precise. When I was offered the job, I took his advice and negotiated a good salary. John and I would become good friends.

About a year earlier at another internship in Boston, my mentor told me to avoid taking entry-level jobs if I knew I could do more challenging work. Specifically, he admonished me, saying, "Whatever you do, don't take a QA job. You are good enough to be a software developer. If you start at the QA level, you'll be typecast, and it will take you longer to move up the ranks to developer." QA stands for Quality Assurance and describes the job of those who test the programs that developers write. QAs would much rather write code than test it. I was a freshman when I received this advice. It was my first exposure to the absurdity of the caste system in many large technology companies.

I eventually left the job that John helped me get in Atlanta. Corporate politics and egos began to inhibit my growth, and I was not willing to wait around until things improved. I also became frustrated working for someone who made multiple times as much as I did. I knew that my talents were worth more than any company was willing to pay me. A few months after I left the job, I founded my company.

What does this have to do with being an entrepreneur? If you are currently still working, it means everything. So many potential entrepreneurs don't know their worth. They are paralyzed by their comfort, unwilling to maximize their true potential. If only they would wake up and realize that their salary is only a fraction of what they could earn as entrepreneurs. Fortunately, I woke up early.

Once you have taken the leap to become an entrepreneur and you have been in business for a while, knowing your worth takes on another meaning. At this point, it's not about *your* worth necessarily; it's about your company's worth. There is no better example of someone who understood his company's worth than Mark Zuckerberg, cofounder and CEO of Facebook.

Mark Zuckerberg's company had several opportunities to be acquired once it really began to grow. For example, Viacom offered $75 million to buy the entire company in 2005. It wanted to combine Thefacebook, as it was called then, with MTV.com. As chronicled in David Kirkpatrick's book *The Facebook Effect*, "If Zuckerberg accepted such an offer, he would have put about $35 million in his pocket for a year's work. But that didn't matter to him." Most of us would have taken the offer. Zuckerberg thought his company would be a billion-dollar company someday. Seven years later, Facebook's valuation was estimated to be $75 billion right before it went public. Yes, that's billion with a "b."

Whether you are contemplating leaving your job or entertaining offers for the purchase of your company, it takes guts to hold your ground to get what you believe you or your company is worth. You have to understand that things do not always work in your favor, but when they do, it's all worth it. Don't take it from me. Just ask Mark Zuckerberg.

93) You Can't Keep a Job

I didn't see it then, but it turned out that getting fired from Apple was the best thing that could have ever happened to me. . . . It freed me to enter one of the most creative periods of my life.
—Steve Jobs, cofounder, Apple

I have never been able to keep a job for more than five months. I have had five jobs and internships in my life, and most have ended faster than it took to actually secure the opportunity. Most of the jobs were summer internships or short-term positions, but a few were long-term, 9-to-5 jobs. Regardless, I figured out early in life that having a traditional job wasn't for me. Little did I know that my nomadic experience was typical of a budding entrepreneur.

According to a recent study by LinkedIn, a professional social networking site with over 100 million public profiles, entrepreneurs stayed at previous jobs for about 2.5 years compared to the national average of 4.4 years. The study reveals the restless nature of entrepreneurs who cannot stay in any position too long. The desire to move on can come from several sources.

For me, the restlessness came from the inability to drop my own projects. I always had an idea or business that I was developing, and that was my priority. I felt that working a job instead of working on my own business was a bad choice. No matter how enticing the job was, I always ended up choosing my own projects. Even when my employer allowed me to work on my own projects, I eventually left because work was taking away from the precious time I could devote to pursuing my own ideas. Having a job was not helping me to grow. It was nothing more than a paycheck and a sense of financial security. For most people, that's enough, but I wanted something different, something more.

Some of the most famous entrepreneurs couldn't keep a job either. One of my favorite reject stories is how billionaire Mark Cuban, founder of MicroSolutions and owner of the NBA's Dallas Mavericks, was fired from his job as a computer salesman. When Cuban failed to open the store on time, his manager fired him immediately. It was Cuban's last job. In fact, Walt Disney, Oprah Winfrey, Michael Bloomberg, J. K. Rowling, Thomas Edison, Bernie Marcus, and Arthur Blank were all fired, too, before they became fearless entrepreneurs. They would all go on to build billion-dollar enterprises. Many of these moguls still identify getting fired as one of the best things that ever happened to them and believe that the experience ignited in them a fire to follow their own path to success.

There are many signs that you are an entrepreneur, but not being able to keep a job for long is perhaps the biggest sign. If you can't hold down a job, the cosmos may be trying to tell you something. Instead of running from job to job, run full force into your entrepreneurial destiny. I did, and I have had a "job" for over twelve years straight.

94) You Cry When Things Don't Go Your Way

Disappointment is an endless wellspring of comedy inspiration.
—Martin Freeman, English actor

There's no crying in business! Well, that's what I thought until I read the Steve Jobs biography that came out shortly after his death.

To my surprise, it seemed like Jobs cried about everything that didn't go his way. For example, when Jobs was forced out of Apple, the very company he founded, he cried. Apple's board at the time decided to support John Scully as CEO and planned to reduce Jobs's role in the company. Walter Isaacson, author of the biography, wrote, "He [Jobs] went back to his office, gathered his long-time loyalists on the Macintosh staff, and started to cry." This was just one of several examples throughout the book of Jobs crying. A few of the reasons are somewhat justified—like getting kicked out of the billion-dollar company you started—but others seem especially frivolous. Jobs also cried when cofounder Steve Wozniak was deemed employee number one and he was not. He cried when some of his best employees left the company. He cried when negotiations didn't go his way. He cried when his team had design problems. I think you get the watery picture.

I was quick to judge Jobs, but then I remembered that I, too, have cried when things have not gone my way in business. The first and most emotional breakdown took place when I was twenty-five, and a major investment fell through at the last minute. I felt like my world was ending, so I cried. This wasn't a dignified weep when tears slowly well up and finally pour from your eyes, streaming gracefully down your cheeks, when you still have control over your body. No, it was much worse. I cried so hard that I sounded like a toddler who could barely breathe. Mucus was coming out of my nose, and my body jolted rhythmically during inhalation to keep up with the outpouring of raw emotion. Luckily, my supportive girlfriend was there to console, hold, and pray for me and tell me that everything would be just fine. I eventually recovered and felt better because of the waterworks.

When I recalled this incident, I smiled because I knew that Jobs and I were so passionate about our businesses that we couldn't help but express in the most natural way how an adverse situation affected us. Many entrepreneurs internalize their unhappy emotions so as to appear invulnerable. There certainly is a place for that. However, sometimes a good cry is what a CEO needs to move on and to overcome whatever has happened.

Everyone talks about how entrepreneurs should be passionate. However, they rarely talk about being passionate in the most comprehensive sense. Passion manifests itself in different forms, from working long hours to yelling at members of your team, from having youthful enthusiasm to even crying when something doesn't go your way. If you feel the urge to cry every now and then about an issue related to your business, go ahead and cry. It's quite alright. Many entrepreneurs in the world have cried about their businesses. They just aren't honest enough to admit it like Jobs and me.

95) It's Never Too Late to Be an Entrepreneur

You are never too old to set another goal or to dream a new dream.
—C. S. Lewis, author, theologian

"I'm too old to start a business," said my forty-four-year-old friend when I encouraged her to become an entrepreneur. I shook my head as she rambled on about how she has too many responsibilities and how she's not as creative as she used to be. Her excuses were ridiculous, but all too common for people her age.

As the media focus on young CEOs like Facebook's Mark Zuckerberg and Instagram's Kevin Systrom, it is easy to assume that most companies these days are started by teenagers and people in their twenties. Consequently, many older people buy into this media hype and think that starting a company is for young people, accepting that their chances of success are limited by their age. This assumption and the media hype couldn't be further from the truth.

First, the media hype is heavily focused on the technology sector, which tends to glorify young superstars. When it comes to what is most appealing to the media, the new social media company always overshadows the new bakery on Main Street. However, most new businesses in the United States aren't tech-related and sexy. They will be primarily sole proprietorships and small businesses with fewer than five employees. Most of their owners will be old enough to be a tech guru's mother or father.

Second, older people are starting more businesses than people in their teens and twenties. According to a Kauffman Foundation study, Americans between the ages of thirty-five and forty-four represented the largest increase in entrepreneurial activity from 2008 to 2009. Americans between ages fifty-five and sixty-four constituted the second-largest jump. The reasons range from middle-aged adults wanting to supplement their income to retired individuals wanting to continue working. Regardless of the reasons, older Americans are catching the entrepreneurial bug, which is good news for everyone. Unfortunately, we don't hear enough about these exciting data.

Interestingly, research shows that older people are more likely to be successful when they start businesses. Older entrepreneurs have the experience needed to better navigate the rough waters of entrepreneurship. During years of work, they have developed a treasure chest of skills that makes them highly valuable. For instance, if they go into business in the same industry in which they worked for many years, their understanding of the business is a tremendous competitive advantage.

In other good news, University of Chicago economist David Galenson contends that "experimental innovators" require time to reach their peak. His research, which is largely credited with cracking the code of the creative mind, concludes that experimental innovators do their best work in life at an older age. They accomplish their genius through trial and error. Examples of these innovators are Steve Jobs, Mark Twain, and Alfred Hitchcock.

Older people may give a bunch of reasons for saying they are too old to start a business, but they are just excuses, many of which are defended with misinformation. Now we have plenty of data and reasons to support why being in your later years is an asset, not a liability, when starting a business. If you are in your early thirties, forties, or older, it is not too late to start a business. Don't let your age deter you from pursuing your dream. Ultimately, a solid business idea paired with flawless execution, not a fresh face, is what leads to success in business.

96) You Feel Unequaled Joy When Your Idea Becomes Reality

"It's alive!"
—Dr. Frankenstein, in *Frankenstein*

After launching my website as a college sophomore, I used to go to the campus computer labs of different schools and set the default website of the browsers to my site. Doing this was not only an effective way to introduce the website to students, but it also allowed me to witness how students reacted to seeing and to using the site for the first time.

Most of the first-time visitors were surprised to discover a professional-looking website that creatively showcased their schools with news, photos, and video. In fact, some students who came to the lab with their friends would immediately share the website with the people who came with them. They were that excited. Meanwhile, I observed the students navigating my website—noticing what they clicked on, how long they stayed on the site, and what expressions they had on their faces. Many students stayed on the site for a long period of time, clicking through the photo galleries, chatting with friends, browsing personals, and enjoying the site's features.

As the site grew in popularity, I saw more students using it. Being able to watch people use and enjoy something I created was especially gratifying and gave me a sense of joy that I had never experienced. Often when you come up with an idea, it doesn't always work in the real world the way you envisioned it would. I didn't have that problem. I got it right the first time.

Likewise, when I launched my magazine a few years later, I watched readers flip through the pages. Again, I had a hit with the magazine as readers all around Atlanta loved it and anticipated the arrival of the next issue. I felt the same joy that I received from watching users browse the website.

Perhaps the most joy came from receiving positive feedback from viewers of my website, readers of my magazine, and eventually users of my software products. The feedback that I remember most came from a mother whose daughter was in France as an exchange student during the terrorist attacks of September 11, 2001. She wrote me a poignant letter describing how her daughter viewed my website often to stay connected with her school and country. It was a difficult time for her young daughter while she was in Europe, and visiting my website enabled her to escape the anti-American sentiment she received at the time. The mother was truly grateful and moved enough to write me a thank-you letter. I was elated to know that my website served as an emotional haven for her daughter, something I never would have imagined.

What do these anecdotes have to do with being an entrepreneur? They exhibit the fact that entrepreneurs take immense pride and joy in transforming their idea into reality. Knowing that your idea actually works and has impacted the world in some way is a feeling like no other. For many, it's even a greater feeling than making the first sale or receiving the first payment.

I am reminded of the overwhelming sense of joy that the character Dr. Emmett Brown—affectionately known as Doc—displays in one of my favorite movies, *Back to the Future*. When Doc realizes that his time machine works, he is speechless for a few seconds, in a state of euphoric amazement. Then he dances down the street as if no one is watching. It's moments like this and the ones I shared that motivate entrepreneurs to create; moments like these make our enterprising pursuits that much more special.

97) Following Your Passion Is Bogus

If passion drives you, let reason hold the reins.
—Benjamin Franklin, entrepreneur; Founding Father, United
States of America

One particular three-word phrase has become the mantra of entrepreneurs everywhere, used to inspire and to motivate the oppressed masses to liberate themselves from their chains of dispassion.

"Follow your passion." Another version is the following: "Do what you love." Any variation of this phrase has the same questionable assumption. It assumes that success comes from emotional satisfaction or from engaging in an activity for which you have a strong liking or desire, the very definition of passion. Considering that success in entrepreneurship is having a profitable business, this assumption is far from the truth. Contrarily, success comes from doing that which often gives you the least emotional satisfaction.

Despite this reality, many seasoned entrepreneurs perpetuate the passion myth when discussing how to be successful in business. Studies show that it is much easier to inspire and to motivate through positive reinforcement, but this approach undermines the importance of doing what's difficult and uncomfortable on a consistent basis to propel a business forward. Instead of emphasizing that people do what they love, we should at least draw equal attention to the need to tackle with the same energy the things they hate.

What do I mean by "hate"? When you have a business, especially a young business, you inevitably find yourself doing things that are not enjoyable. Whether it's making cold calls to generate more business or firing an unproductive employee, these unpleasant tasks are key to staying on the right path. The strongest and wisest entrepreneurs learn to assume these tasks diligently and without fail.

Recently, business mogul Mark Cuban caused quite a stir when he published a blog post that added a different take on the passion myth. Known for speaking his mind, Cuban wrote,

"Follow Your Passion" is easily the worst advice you could ever give or get. . . . There are always going to be things we love to do. That we dream about doing. That we really really want to do with our lives. Those passions aren't worth a nickel. . . . If you really want to know where your destiny lies, look at where you apply your time. . . . Don't follow your passions, follow your effort.

Cuban's perspective, which is different but equally valid, was the result of an honest assessment of the fallacy that money, happiness, and success magically appear when you follow your passion.

Entrepreneurs shouldn't necessarily be encouraging people to follow their passion to attain success in business. This advice is more applicable to a lofty self-help goal in life. Business is about solving problems, improving the quality of life, creating new solutions, and yes, making money. These things involve a great deal of pain and drudgery, not endless euphoria. If you are able to align building a solid business with doing what you love, that's great, but it certainly isn't a requirement. Likewise, it's a bad idea to try to monetize your passion without extensive consideration. Finally, whether your business has anything to do with your passion shouldn't be the determining factor in why you want to start a business.

98) You Have the Right Motivation

Money was never the motivation.
—Katarina Witt, German figure skater, model

As an entrepreneur develops, so should that person's motivation. In most cases, we talk about motivation in general terms; rarely, if ever, do we place a value judgment on the different types. We assume that all motivation, as long as it catalyzes entrepreneurial activity, is acceptable. Or we assume that most entrepreneurs are ultimately motivated by money. (The goal of business, after all, is to make a profit.) However, these common assumptions do not help us delineate and value the different types of motivation, which can be used to examine an entrepreneur's success or failure—and progress or retrogress—at a given moment. For example, entrepreneurial motivation varies in intensity, validity, and sustainability. To better explain these degrees of difference, I have formed a context or framework that attempts to explain the natural maturation of a typical entrepreneur's motivation in three basic stages along with some of their challenges.

1. *The first level of motivation has to do with one's desire to leave or to avoid a job because of unsatisfactory conditions*, whether it's a demanding workload, little freedom, difficult colleagues, lack of opportunity, or low pay. While employed, this future entrepreneur wishes to leave a job but has an unwillingness or hesitation to forfeit some of the comforts of employment. These comforts may include a lack of responsibility, a steady paycheck and benefits, or a sense of security.

This level is the least mature and organic motivation for entrepreneurship. The motivation comes from an urge to get away or to escape, not to solve a business problem. Besides, other jobs can always offer a better experience and thus alleviate unsatisfactory conditions. In the case that a person finds such an accommodating job, the urge to pursue entrepreneurship subsides. Furthermore, this person is likely pursue entrepreneurship to re-create a similar environment to the one just abandoned, but on one's own terms. This entrepreneur is working to restore a level of comfort. Therefore, entrepreneurs who are at this level rarely go beyond self-employment or sole proprietorship and opt for lifestyle entrepreneurship. Regardless, when the courage comes to leave the job and to start a business, the motivation goes to the second level.

2. *The second level of motivation deals with survival*, and is perhaps the most natural level of the three. This motivation is in-

grained in us as humans. Still, an entrepreneur who escaped the confines of a 9-to-5 will struggle to grow accustomed to this new motivation, especially in going from an employee mentality to an entrepreneur mentality. While entrepreneurs eat only what they kill, employees eat regardless of what they kill. While entrepreneurs don't expect a steady paycheck, employees know exactly how much they will earn and when that amount will be paid. While entrepreneurs believe that the potential of their company is greater than the compensation from any job, employees define their potential within the confines of their company. Most importantly, entrepreneurs are motivated by an intrinsic sense of survival, and employees are motivated by an extrinsic sense of entitlement.

This level presents a unique but understandable problem for entrepreneurs. I call it the "subsistence entrepreneurship" problem. Entrepreneurs motivated primarily by survival or by maintaining a certain standard of living often don't exceed the efforts needed to meet these goals. As a result, their businesses hardly grow. Entrepreneurs may start new, promising ventures, but inevitably their growth is limited by their own efforts or lack of ambition to overachieve. Entrepreneurs at this level must devise a clever growth strategy and goals that pull them outside of their new equilibrium. Most entrepreneurs never go beyond this level of motivation.

3. *The third level of motivation has to do with creating a great product or service that meets a need or solves a problem.* As opposed to the previous two levels, only this level finds motivation within the context of the business world. Therefore, this level of motivation is most appropriate and conducive to high achievement.

For example, PayPal was not necessarily created to make global payments and money transfers via the Internet easier. Instead, it stemmed from cofounder Peter Thiel's libertarian beliefs fortified while a college student. PayPal was a solution to the problem of countries, dictators in particular, manipulating currencies and thereby destroying free-market systems. Similarly, Facebook's cofounder Mark Zuckerberg has been driven by a desire to create a great product that makes the world more transparent and connected.

The most revered entrepreneurs of our lifetime have overwhelmingly come from a position of financial privilege, which largely allows them to bypass the first two levels of motivation. For the most part, they do not have to contend with the psychological baggage and limitations of the previous levels. For example, focusing on building a revolutionary product is much easier when you don't need to work a full-time job to eat or pay the bills. Statistics show that most entrepreneurs do not have this advantage.

There certainly are other motivations for becoming an entrepreneur than the three presented here, but they are inferior. The goal of entrepreneurs should be to align their motivation with their business's objective, which is an element of the third and highest level of motivation. Once you achieve this level, your company has the highest potential for greatness.

99) You Love Your Life

The best way to predict the future is to create it.
—Peter Drucker, author, management consultant

Sometimes I have to pinch myself and ask, "Is this for real?" For instance, I recently played eighteen holes of golf on a beautiful private course in Orlando, Florida, with three physicians, some of whom certainly have a net worth in the millions. On the sixteenth hole, one of my major clients called to verify my company's address to send two large checks. At the same time, my various businesses are generating income (I get e-mail alerts about sales figures). Meanwhile, my family is enjoying an extended vacation at Disney World and other attractions around Orlando. Normally, we fly to destinations, but this time we drove because one of my clients gave me a luxury SUV to use for the trip. And that was just one day!

Other pinch-myself moments include being invited by the Norwegian government to stay in the Nobel Prize winner's suite at the Grand Hotel in Oslo, being invited to the White House by President Barack Obama, eating dinner with Kenya's vice president in Nairobi, sitting courtside at an NBA All-Star Game, playing golf with Vice President Joe Biden in St. Thomas, chatting with Kanye West during a private listening party for his new album, and so on. All of these great moments occurred because I had the fortitude to start my own business and to create value for these important individuals and organizations.

The quality of life that I have had as an entrepreneur has been greater than anything I could have imagined. I am especially proud of the fact that my businesses have allowed me to support my growing family as well as the families of those who work for me, to travel the world to over twenty-five countries, to help many charities and causes dear to my heart, and to inspire others to pursue their dreams. If I hadn't caught the entrepreneurial bug during my sophomore year in college about twelve years ago, I would lead a very different, almost certainly less-fulfilling life.

Yes, life is good—and you would probably expect me to tell you that as an evangelist of entrepreneurship—but things haven't always been perfect, and I don't expect them to always be that way.

Life as an entrepreneur has been difficult, too. In some wearisome times I thought I was going to lose it all, wondering if the path that I was following was the right one. I've wanted to give up. In fact, on my worst days, all of these thoughts can cross my mind. However, no matter how down or unsure I have felt, I have always believed that entrepreneurship is the surest way to happiness and to self-actualization. This strong belief is perhaps what pulls me back again and again to start yet another business.

Apparently, I am not the only one who feels this way. I have never met an entrepreneur who hates being an entrepreneur. Regardless of whether they are filing for bankruptcy or preparing for an initial public offering, entrepreneurs love taking risks and starting businesses. For most of them (and me), no other way of life comes close.

Entrepreneurs love their lives not necessarily because of the benefits of success but because we love the game of entrepreneurship, which can bring joy *and* pain. An indescribable feeling of joy comes from knowing that you are in control of your destiny, and this joy is present through the good and the bad times. When I say I love my life, it's neither to gloat nor to boast, but to reaffirm my belief that being an entrepreneur is life at its best. This is what makes entrepreneurs one of a kind.

100) You're an Entrepreneur Forever

"You take the blue pill—the story ends, you wake up in your bed and believe whatever you want to believe. You take the red pill—you stay in Wonderland and I show you how deep the rabbit-hole goes."
—Morpheus, in *The Matrix*

As I grow older, I sometimes imagine how my entrepreneurial drive will change when I reach the age of eighty, ninety, or even one hundred. Will I choose to go into retirement, a life full of rest, travel, and quality time with my grandchildren? Or will I continue to work in search of the next great idea that will generate wealth, working long hours and going into the office? While a leisurely life in retirement is appealing and is the lifestyle most people aspire to when they reach their golden years, I doubt that I will select that option. As I become a centenarian in 2079, I am sure that my entrepreneurial spirit will be just as strong and as ambitious as it is now.

I have learned about the natural, riveting quality of entrepreneurship: Once you catch the bug, it never leaves you. The ambition and will to reach entrepreneurship's highest levels are no match for common obstacles like age or even failure.

Even advanced age doesn't matter. I am inspired by entrepreneurs like Truett Cathy, the ninety-one-year-old founder of the quick-service restaurant Chick-fil-A. Cathy doesn't let old age slow him down. He adheres to his daily routine of getting up early and continues to play an important role in the billion-dollar company he founded sixty-six years ago. In fact, Cathy released a book recently titled *Wealth: Is It Worth It?* in which he discusses the opportunities and responsibility that wealth creates. We can all learn from Cathy's amazing drive at a time when most people his age slowed down long ago.

Likewise, it doesn't matter how disastrous an entrepreneur's last business was. I have yet to meet someone who has totally written off entrepreneurship after failing at it miserably. No matter how terrible their experiences in business, entrepreneurs have the unique ability to separate the results of their endeavors from the sanctity of the concept of entrepreneurship itself. It could also be that the dream of acquiring financial independence and the ability to determine one's own destiny has a strong human appeal.

Muhammad Yunus, microfinance pioneer and Nobel Peace Prize winner, argues that entrepreneurship is as natural to our humanity as is our need to eat.

All human beings are entrepreneurs. When we were in the caves, we were all self-employed . . . finding our food, feeding ourselves. That's where human history began. . . . As civilization came, we suppressed it. We became labor because they stamped us, "You are labor." We forgot that we are entrepreneurs.

Perhaps Yunus is on to something. He seems to have figured out the most primal reason to explain why once you are an entrepreneur you are always an entrepreneur. Or as Yunus might say, "Once you realize your natural state of being as an entrepreneur, you'll never return to viewing yourself as labor."

Regardless of the reason entrepreneurship is so captivating, we can all agree that it is. Even if you return to a 9-to-5 job, you will never view it in the same way. You are just an entrepreneur in hiding or in transition. Those of us who have taken the "red pill" know this already. But if you are considering entrepreneurship for the first time, know that once you are in Wonderland, it is forever. There's no turning back.

Afterword

There is nothing to writing. All you do is sit down at a typewriter
and bleed.
—Ernest Hemingway, author

Thank you for reading my book. I am grateful for your investment of both time and money.

I hope that you have learned many valuable lessons that will inspire you to either start a business with enhanced knowledge or to improve the current business that you have. I encourage you to share this book with others who may also benefit from it.

Furthermore, I hope that this is the beginning of a long-lasting relationship in which I can continue to give you advice, and you can give me feedback. Please follow me on my blog, Twitter, and Facebook. Via these social media outlets, you will find new content, including articles, speaking engagements, and future projects.

Finally, I wish you much success as you continue on the most fulfilling and rewarding journey I know: entrepreneurship.

Kevin D. Johnson
Atlanta, Georgia, USA
Twitter: @BizWizKevin
E-mail: kevin@johnsonmedia.com
Web Site/Blog: TheEntrepreneurMind.com
Facebook: http://www.facebook.com/TheEntrepreneurMind

Acknowledgments

There is no such thing as a 'self-made' man. We are made up of thousands of others.
—George Matthew Adams, American newspaper columnist

When I want to accomplish a goal, I go all in. In other words, I find some way to challenge myself by keeping a grueling schedule for one hundred days to attain my goal; I focus intently. When I ran for political office in 2009 I committed to walking neighborhoods in my district and knocking on doors to get votes for one hundred days in a row. When I wanted to run my first half marathon, I stuck to a rigid schedule that required me to train for about one hundred days. When I wanted to write this book, I decided to write every day for at least one hundred days in a row. I accomplished that goal, and this book is a result of my steadfast efforts.

However, it wasn't as simple as sticking to my one-hundred-day plan and relying on my own ability to make this book a reality. What may seem like an accomplishment achieved on my own is quite the opposite. Through the entire process of putting together this book, I have had much help and encouragement, whether it was from a close family member, a distant friend through social media, or a professional editor. Without their help, this book would have never been published. It would have remained an unattainable dream, something unchecked on my bucket list. I can only hope that my gratitude and acknowledgment in this part of the book are sufficient to express how thankful I am for everyone's help.

First, I must acknowledge God who is my strength and whose glory is the purpose of my desire to succeed in life and in business.

Next, I must thank my parents, Richard and Jean, for being the best parents anyone could have. I am because they are. Thank you for believing in me and supporting my entrepreneurial endeavors. Also, thank you for instilling in my siblings and me a love for books and reading. My mom read to us constantly as children. As we grew older, story time turned into a strong encouragement to read often. I can still hear her admonishing us, "Turn off the TV and read a book!" One of my most vivid memories as a youngster is watching my father read and overhighlight one of his brightly covered study books on the Bible or receiving from him a marked-up book that he recently read on business management. Barely out of middle school, I was reading books about corporate management and leadership.

Furthermore, I owe so much to my wife, Deidre, who gave me the space needed to complete this project from the start. Even with our demanding six-month-old son, she never wavered in her support. Even when our family vacation at Disney World coincided with my final seven days of writing, she encouraged me to finish strong and not to miss even a day. In general, her faithful support for my business and goals in life has been a tremendous blessing. Nothing else can explain her excitement, encouragement, support, and tolerance but unconditional love.

Also, my siblings have been especially encouraging. My older brother, Richard, has been a huge inspiration to me, whether being one of the best jazz pianists in the world or recommending books I should read. In fact, his first recommendation changed my life and my view of just how exciting books can be. In high school, he gave me *Miles Davis: The Autobiography*, a riveting narrative that spawned my love for the autobiography genre and jazz trumpet. My younger sister, Angela, allowed me to borrow her business books from college to improve my finance, accounting, and marketing skills since I wasn't a business major like she was.

Equally supportive have been my extended family and my wife's immediate and extended family. Whether it's through leveraging their networks to help me or simply being my biggest fans, they have all contributed to the success of this book. Special thanks goes to the Turners: Dennis, Janet, Dennise, Donnice, Dawn, and Dorian. Also, I thank the grandparents who have been overwhelmingly supportive.

Undoubtedly, one of the biggest influences in my life was my church family in the Boston, Massachusetts area, where I lived for many years until my senior year in high school. It was a special church group in which several accomplished men and women owned their own businesses and encouraged us youngsters to follow in their footsteps. Many of them were technology entrepreneurs and are still in business to this day. In fact, I sometimes do business with them. There were also lawyers and doctors who owned their own practices. They taught me that starting a business and thriving in what may seem like unfavorable conditions was not only possible, but also expected. Thank you especially to William Bagley, Carlo Cadet, Michael Collison, Michael Dawson, Mr. and Mrs. Larry Edmonds, Tom Farrington, James Grigsby, Jonathan Mayo, Denzil McKenzie, Kevin Pearson, Darrin Poullard, Malcolm Roberts, Michael Robinson, Lyndon Myers, and John Womack. All of you were excellent examples.

I am especially thankful to those of you who have taken the time to read or to preview copies of my book and to give me feedback. Likewise, those of you who follow me on Twitter and read my blog were invaluable during this whole process. Still, thanks to all of you who have provided quotations in support of this project.

These gracious people include Dexter Caffey, Andrew Dietz, Scott Gerber, Vivian Giang, Christopher Hanks, James Herbert, Samuel T. Jackson, Shaun King, Robert Lahm, Kent Matlock, David Meredith, Chau Nguyen, Eric Overby, Devon Wijesinghe, Andrew Young, and others. Your insights, comments, and endorsements have made this a much better book and have given me increased confidence.

There is nothing more humbling and painful than having your manuscript critiqued and edited. It's one of the most humbling experiences I have ever gone through. Nevertheless, it's necessary to make my message clear and effective—and that's a good thing. As a result of going through the editing process, I have become a better writer and communicator. Bob Land, who is a master editor, was invaluable. Thank you so much for your suggestions and expertise.

And finally, I thank all of my colleagues, mentors, and friends who have supported me over the years. I have attempted to list as many of you as possible. If I omit anyone important, I apologize. It certainly wasn't intentional. Thank you to Henry "Hank" Aaron, Donovan Adams, Tiwa Aganga-Williams, Blair Alexander, Amy Allen, Kate Atwood, Shane Aubrey, James Bailey, Antoinette Ball, Leona Barr-Davenport, Gail Banks, Kornelius Bankston, Tony Baraka, Greg and Juanita Baranco, Gerald Barnes, Galen Barrett, Lekan Bashua, Bijan C. Bayne, Danny Bellinger, Kathleen Bertrand, Geoffrey and Beth Bennett, C. J. Bland, Cicely Bland, Robert Bolton, Jasper Boykin, John Breton, Max Brooks, Sierra Brown, Tiffany Bussey, Joshua Butler, Laura Butts, Alzay Calhoun, Jason Carter, Rodrigo Cervantes, Amani Channel, Stacey Chavis, Christopher Cooper, Chris Craft, Gloria da Cunha, Cedric Dark, Anthony Davis, Rachel Bottini Donohoe, Bandon Douglass, Araba Dowell, Ralph Dragon, Torarie Durden, Jason Edwards, Mike Eckert, Marshawn Evans, Tomeeka Farrington, Garry Fielding, Daniel Fowler, Cristina Francis, Howard Franklin, Robert Franklin, Bernice Frazier, Nekeidra Shegog Frederick, Daniel

Gaviria, Lamar Gilliam, Kat Goduco, Joey Gonzalez, Henry Goodgame, J. Craig Gordon, Natasha Gore, Eric Gordon, Garrett Gravensen, Kacey Greene, Russell Griffin, Hezekiah Griggs III, Cynthia Hale, Lori Hall, Milano Harden, Amisha Harding, Malla Haridat, Jeremy Halbert-Harris, Ryan Hattaway, Caroline Hennigar, Rhonda Hight, Derrick Hill, Michael T. Hill, Ebony Hillsman, Michael Holmes, Jacinta Howard, Tom Hughes, Spencer Humphrey, Tad Hutcheson, Markel Hutchins, Carletta S. Hurt, Alicia Ingram, Beverly Isom, Bunnie Jackson-Ransom, Adora Andy Jenkins, Sabrina Jenkins, William Jenkins, Penny Jerald, Gordon Johnson, Karla Johnson, Michael Johnson, John Wayne Jones, Melvin Jones, Felicia Joy, Jamahl L. King, Greg Knight, Joshua Kushner, Sabrina LaFleur, Jeffrey Lam, Donnie Leapheart, Erik Limpaecher, Jennifer Madden, Guy Madison, Hermon Menghisteab, Rubina Malik, Joy Marshall, Walter Massey, Henry Masson, John Maupin, Lee May, Jonathan Mayo, Kevin R. McGee, Sheridan McNeair, David Meredith, Rene Miller, Mecca Moore, Alisha Thomas Morgan, Carla Morrison, Farai Mtetwa, Lori Newman, Sean Norman, Steven Otu, Carlos Overall, Eric Overby, Ronda Penrice, Erica Petri, Michon Pinnix, Bolaji and Tamara Oyejide, Curtis Parker, Vanessa Parker, Kisha Payton, Eric Perrin, John Pitts, Dameon Pope, J. Kevin Powell, Shonika Proctor, Tigner Rand, Alfred Record, Larry and Alea Riley, Sheri Riley, Sidney Robbins, Jinean Robinson, Chelsey Rodgers, Terrance Rogers, Daniel Rubio, Dewey Sadka, Nadya Saib, I'na Saulsbery, Oliver Santana, Broderick Santiago, Mitch Schlimer, Kevin Scott, Tyree Cinque Simmons, Terrance Smalls, Calvin Smith, Levar Smith, Tom Sobczynski, Steve Sparks, Ricardo Spicer, Corey Sutton, Wayne Sutton, Ciji Tatum, Mark Anthony Thomas, Otis Threatt, Rachel Tobin, Garrett Turman, Carmen Turner, Orie Ward, Boyce Watkins, Anthony Webb, Cheryl Weston, Johntrae Williams, Devin White, Tiffany White, Mr. and Mrs. Ronald Whittle, Jamie Wolf, Catherine Woodling, Derrick Woods, Jason Woody, and Andrew Young.

About the Author

K evin D. Johnson, president of Johnson Media Inc. and a serial entrepreneur, has several years of experience leading his multimillion-dollar marketing and communications company that now serves many of the most notable Fortune 100 businesses. As an innovative leader, he has appeared on ABC's *Good Morning America*, CBS, Oprah Radio, and in *The New York Times* and *The Wall Street Journal*. Moreover, he has appeared on CNN frequently.

Before founding his company in 2000, he engineered web applications and produced computer software for leading companies. He was a software programmer for IBM and a webmaster for CNN Interactive. He also worked for Arthur Andersen Worldwide as a business consultant and software developer.

Hailing from Boston, Massachusetts, Kevin attended Morehouse College in Atlanta, Georgia, where he studied computer science as a NASA scholar and Spanish, graduating with honors. While in college, he started Johnson Media Inc., which in 2000 created one of the first online content management systems, called OmniPublisher. He later sold it to a publishing company, earning the distinction as a social media pioneer. Realizing the tremendous opportunity in applying Internet technologies to media and marketing, he decided to focus his business on this growing market.

Recently, Kevin was the director of economic gardening for the Technology Association of Georgia (TAG), one of the nation's largest nonprofit trade organizations for technology. In this role, he was responsible for leading an innovative approach to economic development that focused on providing resources to high-tech businesses located in Georgia's coastal region.

In his spare time, Kevin enjoys volunteering for nonprofits, listening to salsa and jazz, playing piano in his Latin band, reading, golfing, traveling, and running half marathons. He is a member of the Apex Society and a former board member of the Atlanta Business League (ABL). He lives in Atlanta, Georgia, with his wife and son.

Made in the USA
San Bernardino, CA
13 August 2014